MUSICAL PATHWAYS

Edited by
Chris Harrison
and
Lis McCullough

NATIONAL ASSOCIATION
OF MUSIC EDUCATORS

The authors of all chapters have been most generous in contributing to this book and we are very grateful to them. We are very happy to acknowledge the generous support of Rockschool for this publication, which is part of the work of NAME in supporting high-quality music education for all.

Generously supported by

ISBN 978-0-9566545-1-9

Editors: Chris Harrison and Lis McCullough
Cover design by Ad-lib Design Partnership Ltd, Worcester

CONTENTS

Section 4: Da Capo

Foreword

What are our first musical experiences? How do we build on our early experiences? What factors help us to sustain a meaningful engagement in music? What musical pathways are available for young people today? How do these cater for their learning needs? These are all important questions that music educators need to engage with if we are to provide effective support for the musical development of those with whom we work. As this book shows, people's musical pathways are many and varied, and there is no single route to musical achievement or enjoyment. This emphasizes the importance, at a time when some routes are threatened or being closed down, of keeping open as many pathways as possible. I hope that this book will help to raise awareness of the range of possibilities available, and that the stories it contains will provide inspiration for others following their own musical pathways.

I would particularly like to thank all the contributors, many of whom are members of NAME, for sharing their experiences and expertise in such a generous way. We are also extremely grateful to Rockschool for their generous support of this publication.

Sarah Kekus
Chair, National Association of Music Educators
2010–2011

Notes on the contributors

David Ashworth is a freelance education consultant, specializing in music technology. He is project leader for www.teachingmusic.org.uk and a consultant for Musical Bridges. Other recent work has included consultancy for Musical Futures, Trinity/OU, QCDA, BBC, Teachers TV, and CPD design and delivery for SSAT and many LEAs and music services. He is currently leading a number of projects in the north-west of England and elsewhere on the use of ICT in live performance.

Linda Bance is a music educator specializing in music-making with children in their early childhood. She is renowned nationally and internationally for her work promoting music as an essential a part of children's development and wellbeing. Over the past 30 years she has led projects within children's centres, music services and orchestras and lately has successfully published the book *Voiceplay* with Oxford University Press. Linda is currently music education consultant for the CBeebies programme ZingZillas.

Nick Beach is Academic Director at Trinity College London. He studied at Dartington College of Arts, the National Centre for Orchestral Studies and Middlesex Polytechnic. As a peripatetic violin teacher, he pioneered early approaches to whole class instrumental teaching in primary schools. He has held several management posts with UK music services. Nick was closely involved with the development of the KS2 Music CPD Programme in the UK and in that of the Arts Award qualifications. He currently leads on the development of Trinity's qualifications and teacher development programmes worldwide. As a practising musician he is a violinist and conductor.

Kimberley Birrell is a Year 12 student from Carlisle currently studying music, maths and psychology. She plays the flute and piano as well as singing and really wants to learn to play the guitar and saxophone. She also enjoys sports, such as netball and basketball, and never misses watching a Formula 1 race! She loves music and spends a lot of her free time doing something music related, such as singing in Carlisle Cathedral's youth choir and playing in her school's band or orchestra.

Doug Bott is a freelance musician and Assistive Music Technology specialist from Bristol. He has been a Drake Music Associate since 2000, making music accessible to disabled people through music sessions, training, consultancy and project management. He is a performer and composer with Angel Tech, a partner in the 'occasional' independent record label *Brain-gel*, and has worked with a range of other music and arts organizations including Creative Partnerships, Bodies In Flight, Sing Up, Forest of Dean Music Makers and REMIX.

June Boyce-Tillman read music at St Hugh's College, Oxford and worked for 25 years in London schools. She researched a model for the development of children's creativity that later underpinned the inclusion of this area in the National Curriculum. She has published widely in the areas of music, music education and liturgy/spirituality. She is now Professor of Applied Music at the University of Winchester and Director of Postgraduate Research Studies. As a composer she specializes in religious works for orchestras and children, using English folksongs within their structures. She is an ordained priest in the Anglican tradition.

Pamela Burnard is a senior lecturer in Music Education at the Faculty of Education at the University of Cambridge. Teaching music in six primary and secondary schools in England, Australia and the USA prepared the way for teaching undergraduate and postgraduate courses in creativity, music education methods for undergraduate and graduate programmes along with supervision of Masters and PhD students. Alongside an interest in musical creativities in real world practice, teacher and student creativities, Pam is co-editor of the *British Journal of Music Education* and co-convenor of the British Education Research Association Creativity-in-Education Special Interest Group.

Rosie Burt-Perkins is a Research Associate at the Royal College of Music's Centre for Performance Science, where she works widely across music education and psychology. Her particular interests are in the learning cultures of conservatoires, the relationships between music-making and wellbeing, and the career development of conservatoire students. Rosie co-ordinates the Rhythm for Life project, working with conservatoire students to facilitate music-making for beginner older adults, and is currently completing her PhD at the University of Cambridge.

Roger Crocker developed an early interest in music, especially on the piano but also in vocal and choral music. He studied at the Royal Academy of Music, Reading University and London University Institute of Education. He is currently Lead Music Adviser and Head of the Music Service in West Sussex. He still plays, accompanies, conducts and leads choirs and groups every week. He chairs the NAME AIC Focus Group and is chair of the non-musically focused Adventure, Service Challenge Scheme (age 8–14) which is a main provider of applicants for the Duke of Edinburgh Award Scheme.

Edward Cunningham is 14 years old and lives near Guildford, Surrey. He has been a senior chorister in Guildford Cathedral Choir and Head Boy of its choir school, Lanesborough. Edward plays the oboe and the piano and is currently a music scholar at Winchester College.

Leonora Davies has taught at both primary and secondary phases and was Inspector for Music and Music Services in the London Borough of Haringey. She now works as a freelance music education consultant, including for bodies such as Music for Youth, Sing Up and Trinity Guildhall. She was Chair of NAME and the Music Education Council, and a member of the Music Manifesto Steering Group. She has published a wide range of music education materials and is currently working with the Paul Hamlyn Foundation on the Musical Bridges programme. She was awarded an MBE for services to education in 2004.

Kathryn Deane ran community music projects across England before becoming director of Sound Sense in 1995, where she champions the importance of community music and supports community musicians' professional development. She was an author of the Music Manifesto report *Making Every Child's Music Matter*; and is an editorial board member of the International Journal of Community Music. She advises on courses in community music and on major music education initiatives.

James Garnett is subject leader for the secondary music PGCE and GTP at the University of Reading, where he also teaches on the primary BA(Ed) and MA (Instrumental Teaching). He is Chair of NAME in 2011–12. When not at work, James enjoys cycling and kayaking with his wife and two children. He plays the organ at church regularly and sings, plays the viola and composes rather less regularly.

Evelyn Glennie is the first person to successfully create and sustain a full-time career as a solo percussionist. Through overcoming the adversity of profound deafness she has become one of world's most innovative musicians. As an international motivational speaker Evelyn draws on her experiences to captivate and enthral her audiences.

Richard Hallam grew up in Leicester before going to the Royal Academy of Music and Trent Park College of Education. After a career as a freelance trumpet player and musical director, he became Head of Music Service and Curriculum Adviser for Oxfordshire. He chaired the Music Manifesto Steering Group and also worked closely with Darren Henley on the Review of the Funding and Delivery of Music Education. He is currently National Music Education Grant Director. He was awarded an MBE in 2003 for services to music education.

Chris Harrison is a music education consultant whose recent work includes teaching on ITE courses at London Metropolitan and Greenwich Universities, running courses for teachers and young musicians, and writing educational materials. A former teacher and local authority music adviser, he was Chair of NAME in 2006–7 and is currently Managing Editor (Publications) for the association. His musical tastes are wide-ranging and he performs with a number of groups and ensembles. He is particularly interested in the role of improvisation in learning music and in developing musical activities in the community at large.

Tony Haynes has music degrees from Oxford and Nottingham Universities. In the 1970s he was Musical Director of Nottingham Playhouse and Liverpool Everyman and wrote music for all major regional repertory theatres and touring companies including the RSC; taught at Trinity College of Music; wrote *Music in Between* for the Gulbenkian Foundation; and made several BBC jazz series. Co-founder of Grand Union in 1982, he composes most of its music, which has been extensively recorded and broadcast, loves travelling, and heads up projects in places as diverse as Paris, Lisbon, Turkey, Bangladesh, Shanghai and Melbourne.

Jan Holdstock is a teacher, composer and author whose songs are enjoyed by children and teachers around the world. Her many books for schools include the *Earwiggo* series of musical activity books, the *Oxford Primary Music Course* (*Sounds Musical, Sounds Topical*) and the *Oxford Reading Tree Songbook*. Her songs and cantatas include *Celebration, Footprints on the Moon, The Easter Story, In Viking Times* and *A Christmas Welcome*.

Jonathan Kirby is the founder and artistic director of Kagemusha Taiko, who perform nationally and internationally. The youth section of the group, Kagemusha Junior Taiko has also won wide acclaim for excellence. As author of the world's only English-language guide to learning and teaching taiko, as well as the taiko component of the Musical Futures programme, Jonathan is this country's leading authority on taiko in education.

Alexandra Lamont is currently Senior Lecturer in Psychology of Music at Keele University, where she directs masters and PhD programmes in psychology of music, musical development, and music, health & wellbeing. She has researched musical development in many different contexts and with different age ranges, including studies with infants, children and adults. She was a member of QCA's Musical Development Group advising on the National Curriculum in England and has recently undertaken commissioned evaluations of Wider Opportunities and Music Partnership projects.

Dominique Laviolette is from London and has been playing the piano from the age of seven and composing since he was fifteen. Essentially self-taught, he is a composer, pianist and singer in that order. However, he looks forward to being able to write 'I am a music teacher' upon completion of his PGCE at London Metropolitan University, having given up a career in carpentry to study music education.

Julian Lloyd Webber has achieved international fame as a cellist and is widely regarded as one of the most creative musicians of his generation. He has premiered more than 50 new works for cello and has inspired new compositions from composers as diverse as Malcolm Arnold and Joaquin Rodrigo to James MacMillan and Philip Glass. He is a governor of the Southbank Centre and President of the Elgar Society. As leader of In Harmony, Julian is working to promote personal and community development in some of England's most deprived areas through orchestral-based learning and musical experiences.

Bill C. Martin is Yamaha UK's music education manager, leading a new but highly experienced corporate music education department. Bill's early musical experiences helped shape his passion for all kinds of music and his subsequent drive to develop his distinctiveness as a music and music education professional into a personal brand. The Yamaha UK education team's vision reflects Bill's own: engaging more people in music-making, in a way that is both life-enhancing and distinctive, using the Yamaha brand to inspire musicians at every stage on their own musical journeys.

Lis McCullough has worked as a primary class teacher and music advisory teacher and is now an independent music education consultant. Her MA dissertation focused on children's development in composition and her PhD thesis explored primary teachers' beliefs about music. She plays various instruments including bassoon and concertina and was Chair of NAME in 2008–9.

Paul McDowell works in a secondary Special Educational Needs school in London facilitating music activities and is training at London Metropolitan University to teach music in secondary schools. He has experience working musically in mainstream schools and has also volunteered as a Soundbeam practitioner with pupils with profound and multiple learning difficulties, exploring ways of enabling disabled musicians to create music using new Assistive Music Technologies. He looks forward to commencing his Music PGCE year in September 2011.

Alice Nicholls is a musician and music therapy student from South Lincolnshire, currently studying at Anglia Ruskin University. Alice is an accomplished songwriter, multi-instrumentalist and performer, and has recorded three self-penned albums. She is the daughter of Sue Nicholls, author of *Bobby Shaftoe, clap your hands* and other music publications.

Adam Ockelford is Professor of Music at Roehampton University, London, and is the author of *In the Key of Genius: The Extraordinary Life of Derek Paravicini* (Hutchinson, 2007) and *Music for Children and Young People with Complex Needs* (OUP, 2008). Forthcoming titles include *Applied Musicology: Using Zygonic Theory to Inform Music, Education, Therapy and Psychology Research* (OUP, 2011) and *Music, Language and Autism* (Jessica Kingsley, 2012).

Diane Paterson is the Inclusive Music Team Leader for ArtForms—the music and arts service in Leeds—and secretary of the charity YAMSEN: SpeciallyMusic. In both roles she specializes in developing work with music and children with special needs. This includes developing the Gordon Parry Centre—a regional resource offering instruments, books, props and accessible music technology. She is co-author with Victoria Jaquiss of *Meeting SEN in the curriculum: music* (pub. David Fulton) and gives talks and advice around the country. She is the accompanist to Leeds Youth Choir and a fellow of the Royal Society of Arts.

Simon Pitt is chief executive of Rockschool, Europe's only accredited specialist popular music examinations board, and former course director of the BA Commercial Music degree program at the University of Westminster. He is chair of the Music Industry Association education committee, chair of trustees of a Youth Music Action Zone and chair elect of the International Guitar Foundation (IGF). A copyright specialist, he has worked in the music business in a variety of roles from performing musician to corporate marketing for major record companies as well as a spell as an artist manager.

Vanessa Richards works as a curriculum support teacher for music in the Scottish Borders. Interests include the use of Games Based Learning in primary music. Prior to her current post she worked as a primary teacher and instrumental teacher in Lincolnshire. She performed with a number of brass bands, including Foss Dyke and Hammonds Works, but is currently concentrating on teaching although she hopes to continue with brass band performing in the future.

Alison Richardson was born in Hull and grew up in Whitehaven, attending St James Junior School and then Wyndham Comprehensive school. She went to City of Leeds College of Music and then University of Wales Institute Cardiff to complete teacher training. She now works at Trinity School in Carlisle, a large 11–18 school with nearly 2,000 students on roll. She has recently finished an MA in Performing Arts Education at the Liverpool Institute for the Performing Arts gaining a 1st for her dissertation researching the value of music education and the engagement of students.

Jonathan Westrup has been working for Drake Music since 2005 and is currently working as DM Education Associate. This includes delivering accredited music courses in special schools, training teachers and lobbying music organizations. He has also taught music at secondary level and managed arts and music programmes in youth clubs in south Bristol. As a musician, he has recorded and performed widely, ranging from the New Acoustics to projects run by the LPO and the BSO.

Paul Whittaker is the Artistic Director of Music and the Deaf (www.matd.org.uk), the charity he founded in 1988 to help deaf people to gain access to the world of music. Deaf from birth, he leads workshops and gives talks at events across the UK. He was awarded an OBE for services to music in 2007.

Introduction

This book is an exploration of the many ways in which people can develop their musical lives, whether as musicians, teachers, facilitators: professionals or amateurs. It is designed to reflect the theme of the NAME National Conference 2011, by providing insights into the reasons for people's choices, the contexts in which they make them, and the range of opportunities available. It has not been possible in the time available to attempt a comprehensive survey of people involved in all aspects of music and music education. However, we hope that the book will give some impression of the variety of musical pathways that people take, and prompt reflection on your own pathways.

The book is organized into four sections. The first is a series of overview chapters which set the context; the second is based on responses to two surveys—one conducted on the NAME website and the other in a primary school; the third is a collection of individuals' descriptions of their own pathways. Finally, there is a description of a process for charting your own pathways and an invitation to take part in an extended Musical Pathways project.

In the first chapter of **Section 1**, Alexandra Lamont draws on her own experiences and a range of research findings to consider how children initially become engaged with music, before going on to consider the factors that support continued involvement in music-making. She continues with some reflections on music-making in adult life and how we might help to promote a lifelong interest in music. A significant point in young people's musical pathways is the transition from primary to secondary school, when a change of teacher, environment, approach or available resources can have a disruptive effect on their progress. In her chapter, Leonora Davies examines some of these issues before describing in more detail the Musical Bridges project which is working to promote effective transfer strategies that support the musical, educational and personal development of young people as they move from primary to secondary school. Young people's musical pathways are often framed by an accreditation system, such as graded examinations. Nick Beach considers the history of these, and outlines the developing range of accredited pathways which are now being developed in response to the demands of a broader vision of music education today. For those who progress through to higher education, there are still many choices to be made, and arrival at a conservatoire can seem like a new beginning, rather than a culmination of one's endeavours. Rosie Burt-Perkins' research looks at the journeys which led students to their conservatoire courses and examines how their identities and career aims change during their conservatoire lives. An increasing range of choices, whether at school, college or university, is available to prospective pop and rock musicians, and Simon Pitt takes us expertly through the labyrinth, giving some historical background to the present situation and offering some pointers for the future. Choices available to young people with special educational needs and disabilities have also increased, partly due to the development of assistive technologies. Doug Bott and Jonathan Westrup provide an outline of the accessible musical pathways available in this field. Finally,

Kathryn Deane gives us an insight into the lives of community musicians, how their pathways are 'convoluted, multiple and not always clearly signposted', and the blend of experience and qualifications which supports them in their work.

Section 2 begins with an analysis of the online survey conducted by NAME in preparation for the book. We received responses from 85 people, representing a wide range of involvement in music and music education. In this chapter we offer a brief summary of the responses, which we will expand for the NAME website. The responses expand on the themes of the first section, while at the same time showing how important a factor music is in the lives of the respondents, whether they are involved in music professionally or as amateurs. Lis McCullough then describes the results of a project in a primary school which offers some fascinating and revealing insights into children's perceptions of themselves as musicians and their expectations for the future.

Section 3 comprises a series of chapters in which individuals describe their own musical pathways. As suggested earlier, although in no way claiming to have a representative sample across the whole music education arena, we do hope that we have presented a wide and varied range of contributions. We have been fortunate to receive contributions from school students, trainee teachers, teachers, lecturers, advisers and professional musicians. The range of fields in which they are involved includes classical, 'world' and folk musics; mainstream and special needs education; teaching and performing music in concert halls, schools, colleges, universities and the community. Each of them has a unique and fascinating story to tell and we are grateful to them for sharing them with us. For ease of access, we have arranged them in alphabetical order of surname. These musical pathways provide further exemplification of the issues identified in the previous sections.

In **Section 4**, we conclude with Pamela Burnard's description of her research and reflection tool: 'Rivers of Musical Experience'. This is a form of critical incident charting which she has used widely to help people reflect on their own musical pathways. The book ends with a description of the procedure and an invitation to chart your own 'river'.

We are extremely grateful to all the people who have contributed their own pathways, whether as chapters or responses to the questionnaires. Without their contributions, this book would not have been possible. We have found them fascinating and absorbing reading, offering valuable insights into factors which encourage and/or inhibit musical progress. We also thank the authors of the overview chapters for describing often complex pictures with clarity and thoroughness.

If this book shows anything, it is that musical development is a complex process, and that there are no stereotypical routes to musical achievement or sustained engagement in musical activity. For those who are involved in educating or advising others, it is a reminder that there are many routes that people can follow, and that we all need to find our own pathways, according to our particular needs and abilities. The role of the teacher, or the adult, is to listen and facilitate; but it is also important that those embarking upon their musical journeys are aware of the full range of options available, and that this range is maintained so as to cater as far as possible for all needs.

For all that everybody's pathway is unique, when reading this book you will become aware of resonances and connections both between different chapters within this book, and between the accounts in the book and your own musical pathway. We hope that this will add to the overall understanding of the nature of the journeys we undertake as musicians and educators.

Finally, we draw your attention to the NAME website (www.name.org.uk/publications), where you can find appendices to some of the chapters, more information about the questionnaire and an opportunity to add your own musical pathway.

Chris Harrison
Lis McCullough

Section 1

The Broader Picture

The course of true music never does run smooth

Alexandra Lamont

In this chapter, Alexandra Lamont interweaves the story of her own personal pathway in music with relevant research literature from music education and music psychology. She starts at the very beginning by considering children's first encounters with music, moves on to consider the factors that support music-making in childhood and adolescence and how children feel about their own musical pathways, and concludes with some ideas about involvement in music for life.

Musical beginnings

As a five-year-old I remember being very frustrated by not being able to instantly play the recorder that I had been bought for school. At six, without any prompting from me, a piano, left to us by my great aunt, arrived in the house. She had not learned to play herself, but her husband had been an active musician, and she felt the instrument should stop gathering dust in her flat and find good use elsewhere. I was sent for lessons to the nearest local teacher, a couple of doors down the road, who turned out to be a former concert pianist who also taught at Trinity College of Music in London. She was a hard taskmaster and often made other children cry, but we got on well, I made rapid progress, and there began my real interest in music.

As clearly illustrated by the stories told by me and others in this volume, there are many different routes into music or starting points for musical narratives. From a research perspective, however, these are not well understood. McPherson and Davidson (2006) provide a useful description of some of the factors involved in the process of starting to play a musical instrument, but there is very little research on how this actually happens. While certain factors have been identified, such as talent, motivation and support, chance can also often play a role (McPherson & Williamon, 2006), as in my own case. To try to disentangle some of these factors, it is helpful to consider the different views expressed by children, teachers and parents about what, and who, music is for.

Children themselves express very positive attitudes towards music and learning a musical instrument, and the proportion of children who currently learn is stable, at around a third across primary and secondary school in England (Lamont, Hargreaves, Marshall & Tarrant, 2003). If they are not already doing so, another third of children say they would like to learn an instrument. However, this enthusiasm declines as children get older, with around a quarter of 11-year-olds but less than 5% of 14-year-olds thinking they would be likely to start learning an instrument (Cooke & Morris,

1996). Children appear to be primarily inspired by perceived enjoyment: for example, 7- and 8-year-olds say they began to learn an instrument because it looked like it would be fun, exciting, or enjoyable (McPherson, 2001; McPherson & Davidson, 2002). When musically active adults reflect back on their motivations to become involved with music in childhood, the most important factor is similarly reported as the love of music (Lamont, in press). Finally, for most children, the simple fact of playing a musical instrument (irrespective of ability, talent or skill) defines a person as a musician (Lamont, Hargreaves, Marshall & Tarrant, submitted).

The lack of discourse on talent amongst children and the emphasis on hard work as the basis for achievement (Austin & Vispoel, 1998) is very encouraging. As Gemma, in Year 6, explains for us:

> Anyone can be a musician because if they try they can do it, if you try to play an instrument you'll probably be able to do it, but otherwise, if you don't try you'll never know. (Lamont *et al.*, submitted)

This inclusive attitude chimes with current English government policy, which, since David Blunkett's pledges in 2001, has focused on opening up musical opportunities through schemes such as Wider Opportunities Whole Class Instrumental and/or Vocal Tuition (DfES/DCMS, 2004, 2006). In this, primary school children receive a year of class lessons on an instrument or the voice, with the goal being to stimulate later engagement with music. At the conclusion of the year, children are expected to have developed an interest in music which can be expressed and taken forward in different ways, and preliminary evidence suggests that this approach has the power to transform children's and teachers' attitudes (Bamford & Glinkowski, 2010) as well as the musical cultures of schools (Lamont, Daubney & Spruce, in press).

Bamford & Glinkowski provide an interesting quote from a music coordinator on the issue of inclusion in Wider Opportunities:

> In the first group you watched there were a lot of children with special needs and they're not ones I would have suggested to their parents could do music. But one of them is getting it right all the time and it never occurred to me to think that he would be so coordinated, but he can do it. And he was answering questions and knew that there were three beats in the bar. Educationally, he's significantly behind where he should be for his age. (Bamford & Glinkowski, 2010: 116)

This highlights the well-established folk belief about musical talent that many teachers and parents hold. Outside schemes such as Wider Opportunities, many pupils are still being selected for music tuition using tests of musical ability such as the Bentley or the Wing tests, which embody the notion that musical ability is somehow predetermined. While researchers have provided a raft of evidence counter to this view (Howe, Davidson & Sloboda, 1998; McPherson & Williamon, 2006), pointing out that musical ability is a result of factors such as practice, effort and self-efficacy rather than a necessary precursor to success, these views are nonetheless very pervasive. Both children and adults define themselves in relation to others in music (Lamont, 2002;

Ruddock & Leong, 2005), just as they do in many other fields, and a negative musical identity can lead some children to refuse to engage with music.

In my early research into musical identity, I found that even when all children had opportunities to play musical instruments in the classroom, as guaranteed through the National Curriculum Programme of Study for Music in the early 1990s, not all children defined themselves as musicians (Lamont, 2002). Children's responses were partly affected by their school context. Those from schools where there were very few children taking extra-curricular music tuition were *more* likely to define themselves positively as musicians, while those not having lessons in schools where a large proportion of other children were having lessons were more likely to adopt a negative stance and define themselves as non-musicians. Developing a positive or negative musical identity may be an important part of what sustains children when the going gets tough, so we now move to consider the important issue of continuing to be involved with music.

Continuing with music in childhood

Alongside a conventional musical pathway on the piano (working my way through graded examinations, studying theory, and taking part in festivals and recitals), I also began learning the violin. This path was much less smooth; I started three times over a period of five years, with different teachers, and only persevered eventually aged 13 when I gained a place at Trinity's Junior Department where it was a requirement to be learning two instruments. I chose the instrument strategically to allow me to join in (it was a lot easier to be at the back of the second violins in the orchestra than to be one of the good wind players), rarely practised, and did not particularly take to the repertoire, and I carried on playing only because circumstances dictated. However, by the time I left school I had reached Grade 6 and had begun to enjoy the large orchestral playing with which I was involved.

There has been considerable research effort devoted to understanding why children and young people continue to learn instruments or, conversely, why they may give up. We can follow through the talent account as one potential explanation as, if musical talent does exist, it should be useful as a predictor of success or of ease of progress. More talented children, according to this explanation, might not need to try as hard in order to make progress with music. Some of the young people in our studies agree with this, as Emma, in Year 9, explains:

> To a certain extent it is talent, I think. I'm not trying to be . . . I'm just saying that anybody who does have an instrument, some people can't do it. Some people, I don't know, they just pick it up and cannot play. Even though they've been through the same kind of teaching as others. Some people just find it easier. (Lamont *et al.*, submitted)

These beliefs reflect what Dweck (2000) terms a fixed belief in one's own abilities. Such a belief can be beneficial for those children who feel they are talented in encouraging them to continue, at least in the short term, but conversely can lead some children to give up too quickly. Jo (Year 6) explains this:

I am no good. My cousin tried to teach me the recorder, and she tried for about a week . . . We all had a recorder, and we were all playing, and we all went one at a time, and I was last, and everyone was just going and it came to me and I was out of tune. Everyone was in tune and I was out of tune. (Lamont *et al.*, submitted)

Jo, like many other beginners, has adopted a position of what Dweck calls 'learned helplessness'; she has no confidence in her own abilities, and this has dented her enthusiasm to continue trying to make music. A more adaptive belief structure can result from adopting a concept of incremental ability: irrespective of the starting point, people with this view believe that they can influence their own development by working hard. O'Neill and Sloboda (1997) found that children with this 'mastery' attitude made more progress in the first year of learning an instrument than those who adopted a position of learned helplessness. Sloboda *et al.* (1996) showed that exceptional performers had spent considerable amounts of time practising and putting effort in to achieve success, and most children in our study felt that musical success was entirely down to effort and hard work (Lamont *et al.*, submitted).

In addition to personal factors such as individual motivation and learning style, environmental factors such as context, opportunity, and others are also important in shaping children's and young people's developing self-concepts as musicians (McPherson & Williamon, 2006). The role of teachers has long been recognized (Davidson, Moore, Sloboda & Howe, 1998), but more recent studies have highlighted how parents can also provide important support (Creech, 2009; McPherson, 2009), and Creech has also shown the importance of considering the interactions between teacher, parent, and learner. Musically active adults also highlight wanting to fit in, pleasing parents, or because parents and teachers wanted them to as other important factors which influenced their initial involvement in music and supported them to continue in childhood (Lamont, in press). Thus other people can provide powerful encouragement, and in adolescence the emphasis tends to shift from parents and parent-like teachers to teachers who set high standards and challenging tasks (Davidson *et al.*, 1998). External support thus helps children and adolescents in undertaking useful activities such as practising effectively (Hallam, 1998; McPherson, 2001), which also underpins success.

One danger during the school years is that the opportunities provided for children to engage in music actively do not match their own musical taste. Adolescents in particular are aware of the differences between themselves as largely music listeners and the more formal elements of being a performing musician (Stålhammar, 2003), and there is a well-documented gulf between the kind of music children like to listen to out of school and the repertoire provided at school (e.g. Griffin, 2009). While formal music education tends to be concerned with the kinds of music-making that require support from an adult or more competent older person, it is important not to lose sight of the fact that many children develop highly sophisticated musical identities and engage in activities that do not require formal instruction (Green, 2002), and also to recognize that there are other routes to engaging with music than formal instrumental tuition. Around a third of the children we surveyed (Lamont *et al.*, 2003) said they were not interested in learning an instrument, but they still enjoyed music at school and all of them listened to many hours of music at home.

Becoming a musician

At the age of 13, my musical identity was more clearly developed, and music became my major out-of-school activity. In part this was cemented by the opportunity of going to a junior music college, where I formed new and lasting friendships with my musically-involved peers. Subsequently I went on to study music at university, run the college music society, and continue performing on the piano and violin and as a member of the chapel choir.

When considering what children think of as the defining feature of someone who 'does' music, they give a simple answer: a musician is someone who plays a musical instrument. Note that 'or sings' is not automatically added to this definition, counter to current music education terminology—as Pippa, in Year 6, explains for us, a musician is '. . . somebody who plays music on a musical instrument. I don't think . . . I have never thought a musician is someone who sings, that's not a musician, that's a singer' (Lamont *et al*., submitted).

However, underpinning this apparently simplistic conception, children hold many different perspectives on what they think being good at music means, with a broad range of influential factors (*ibid*.). These include musical skills, such as the ability to play an instrument or make a good sound; performance skills, such as being able to stand up on stage and put on a good show; teaching skills; listening skills; and non-musical skills such as perseverance and effort. Decisions about whether or not to engage with music in formal education may be shaped by the set of beliefs that children and young people hold about music; this raft of reasons for success corresponds to the complexity of the assessment criteria at higher levels of English education and may be responsible for the low take-up of qualifications such as GCSE (Lamont & Maton, 2008).

The multifaceted nature of musical identity is also expressed by adolescents (Stålhammar, 2003), and these distinctions continue to be important when adults are considering their musical identities (Ruddock & Leong, 2005). When thinking about singing, some adults self-define as 'tone deaf' while also describing themselves as 'musical' (Sloboda, Wise & Peretz, 2005), suggesting that a different identity can be constructed as a singer (singing being the facet to which tone-deafness typically refers) and as someone who enjoys music. As noted earlier, there are many different ways in which one can become a musician, and in the final section we consider how musical involvement might be sustained beyond childhood and beyond formal education.

Continuing with music in adulthood

Having graduated with a music degree and with many years of musical training under my belt, when I left university I completely stopped being musically active. Despite going on to higher level study and later a research and teaching career in music psychology, focusing on understanding how children develop musically, at this point in my life I defined myself as a 'former' musician—adopting a similar understanding of the concept of a musical identity as the school children I was researching at the time, because I was not currently playing an instrument. At this point my musical self-concept was almost entirely governed by circumstance and environment: I did not think of myself as a 'failed' musician, or as lacking in ability or skill, but I simply stopped making music.

There are many critical moments in people's musical life stories. An early one for children in the English school system can be the transition from primary to secondary school, a phase with many structural changes and one where many children drop out (Sloboda, 2001). The pressures of a new academic environment and the opportunities to engage in other activities all present challenges to the developing musician's fledgling identity, although in some cases children find the change of environment provides an impetus for more engagement with more meaningful forms of music-making (Marshall & Hargreaves, 2007). Later on, young people often find transitions to different stages of education such as university or college and leaving home and entering the workplace as other critical moments where musical involvement may not be sustained, with still further pressures throughout adult life such as job stress and changes in family situation (Lamont, 2012).

Some research has begun to address the factors that might be necessary to support involvement over long time periods. Davidson and Burland (2006) found that continued involvement through to a professional music career was only possible amongst those who, as adolescents and young adults, both had positive experiences with other people and institutions and had developed methods for coping; these combined to enable them to develop music at the heart of their self-concept. Thus the idea of a musical identity that persists throughout life can be seen to be essential. They describe one such professional, Daniel:

> The emotional and psychological connection that Daniel felt with music may have been a key factor in motivating him to be a musician. Through his experiences at the specialist music school and the key support from his parents, he began to discover his own identity and this was focused around himself as a musician, being someone who loved music. Within this framework, he seemed to have developed strategies for coping with the negative experiences. (Davidson & Burland, 2006: 482)

Conversely, others who had had similarly positive experiences with other people in childhood and adolescence but who had not developed a robust self-concept were more likely to have turned away from pursuing music professionally. Interestingly, however, many of them were still musically active as amateurs, and although Davidson and Burland categorize these people as having failed at their professional objectives they still continue to be active musicians in a different way.

Music education often conceptualizes development as a single pathway, as embodied in the 'pyramid' model in the recent Henley report (Henley, 2011) where all children begin and as time goes on fewer children are able to access and participate. Yet the above research shows that there is no single route to developing a lifelong interest in music. As Lonie and Sandbrook (2011) found from discussions with music educators, musicians, academics and policy makers, 'young people travel on individual musical journeys. Sometimes it might be useful in guiding those journeys to refer to well established routes and pathways, but the routes and pathways should not themselves determine the journeys.'

Ending on a positive note

I came back to music after a break of 14 years when my interest was reignited by attending a week-long classical music festival as an audience member, where I had the chance to talk to the musicians as well as observing masterclasses and concerts. It felt like coming home and, when I did go back home, I mentioned it to a student and friend who suggested I should join the university orchestra. Although the violin was not my first instrument and I had had a shaky start and never achieved very much, I found it relatively straightforward to pick up and play (after restringing!). I started at the back of the second violins, terrified at every rehearsal, and panicked into practising far more than I ever had as a child or adolescent. After a few years and a great deal of improvement, I bought a new instrument and progressed to become the leader of my section.

My latest step in my own musical journey is echoed by many other adults involved in amateur music-making (Lamont, 2012). Many of my survey respondents were currently making music in many different ways, with no clear trajectory apparent from different stages in their lives. However, they had a clear interest in music that was traceable to influences in childhood. Pitts (2009) also found this aspect of meandering routes in adult music participation, and has suggested that a combination of home and school influences in childhood might be the ideal set of factors to promote lifelong engagement with music. However, since there is a very broad range of potential pathways in music, many different interventions can determine the range of journeys through different forms of musical involvement (Lonie & Sandbrook, 2011).

Adults' motivations to return to music after a break often emphasize the technical and challenging aspects of music-making alongside pleasure and enjoyment (Lamont, 2012). They mention the importance of having gained musical skills in childhood, even if they have subsequently changed instruments or styles and, in particular, many reported that having learned to read music provided them with the opportunity to re-engage in various ways. This mirrors findings with 11-year-olds who said they would have liked to learn music notation in primary school to help them take part in what was on offer in secondary school (Marshall & Hargreaves, 2007), and points to the importance of providing a full range of opportunities at different educational stages in order not to limit people's musical horizons.

The final feature that emerged very strongly from these adults was their burning motivation to find a musical pathway; while they might have lost their way at different points, this passion for music kept them searching for a path. To stretch the metaphor, better signposting and more potential routes (from motorways to country lanes) will help more of us achieve our musical potential.

References

Austin, J.R. & Vispoel, W.P. (1998) How American adolescents interpret success and failure in classroom music: Relationships among attributional beliefs, self-concept and achievement. *Psychology of Music*, 26: 26–45.

Bamford, A. & Glinkowski, P. (2010) *'Wow, it's music next' Impact evaluation of Wider Opportunities Programme in Music at Key Stage Two*. Federation of Music Services. www.thefms.org [accessed 20.07.2011].

Cooke, M. & Morris, R. (1996) Making music in Great Britain. *Journal of the Market Research Society*, 28(2): 123–134.

Creech, A. (2009) Teacher-parent-pupil trios: A typology of interpersonal interaction in the context of learning a musical instrument. *Musicae Scientiae,* XIII(2): 163–182.

Davidson, J.W. & Burland, K. (2006) Musician identity formation. In: G. McPherson (ed.) *The child as musician: A handbook of musical development* (pp. 475–490). Oxford: Oxford University Press.

Davidson, J.W., Moore, J.W., Sloboda, J.A. & Howe, M.J.A. (1998) Characteristics of music teachers and the progress of young instrumentalists. *Journal of Research in Music Education*, 46: 141–160.

DfES/DCMS (2004) *Music Manifesto Report No. 1*. London: Department for Education and Skills/ Department for Culture, Media and Sport.

DfES/DCMS (2006) *Music Manifesto Report No. 2: Making Every Child's Music Matter*. London: Department for Education and Skills/Department for Culture, Media and Sport.

Dweck, C.S. (2000) *Self-theories: Their role in motivation, personality and development*. Philadelphia, PA: Psychology Press.

Green, L. (2002) *How popular musicians learn: A way ahead for music education*. Aldershot: Ashgate.

Griffin, S.M. (2009) Listening to children's music perspectives: in- and out-of-school thoughts. *Research Studies in Music Education*, 31(2): 161–177.

Hallam, S. (1998) The predictors of achievement and dropout in instrumental tuition. *Psychology of Music*, 26(2): 116–132.

Henley, D. (2011) *Music Education in England*. London: Department for Education/ Department for Culture, Media & Sport.

Howe, M.J.A., Davidson, J.W. & Sloboda, J.A. (1998) Innate talents: Reality or myth? *Behavioral and Brain Sciences*, 21: 399–443.

Lamont, A. (2002) Musical identities and the school environment. In: R.A.R. MacDonald, D.J. Hargreaves & D.E. Miell (eds.), *Musical Identities* (pp. 41–59). Oxford: Oxford University Press.

Lamont, A. (in press) The beat goes on: Music education, identity, and lifelong learning. *Music Education Research*.

Lamont, A., Daubney, A. & Spruce, G.J. (in press) Singing in primary schools: Case studies of good practice in whole class vocal tuition. *British Journal of Music Education*.

Lamont, A., Hargreaves, D.J., Marshall, N.A. & Tarrant, M. (2003) Young people's music in and out of school. *British Journal of Music Education*, 20(3): 229–241.

Lamont, A., Hargreaves, D.J., Marshall, N.A. & Tarrant, M. (submitted) Musical identities at school. *Psychology of Music*.

Lamont, A. & Maton, K. (2008) Choosing music: Exploratory studies into the low uptake of music GCSE. *British Journal of Music Education*, 25(3): 267–282.

Lonie, D. & Sandbrook, B. (2011) *'Ingredients' for encouraging the talent and potential of young musicians*. Poster presented at the SEMPRE conference on The Developing Musician, Reading, 5 March.

Marshall, N.A. & Hargreaves, D.J. (2007) Crossing the humpback bridge: primary-secondary school transition in music education. *Music Education Research*, 9(1): 65–80.

McPherson, G.E. (2001) Commitment and practice: Key ingredients for achievement during the early stages of learning a musical instrument. *Bulletin of the Council for Research in Music Education*, 147: 122–127.

McPherson, G.E. (2009) The role of parents in children's musical development. *Psychology of Music*, 37(1): 91–110.

McPherson, G.E. & Davidson, J.W. (2002) Musical practice: Mother and child interactions during the first year of learning an instrument. *Music Education Research*, 4: 143–158.

McPherson, G.E. & Davidson, J.W. (2006) Playing an instrument. In: G.E. McPherson (ed.), *The child as musician: A handbook of musical development* (pp. 331–51). Oxford: Oxford University Press.

McPherson, G.E. & Williamon, A. (2006) Giftedness and talent. In G.E. McPherson (ed.), *The child as musician: A handbook of musicial development* (pp. 239–256). Oxford: Oxford University Press.

O'Neill, S.A. & Sloboda, J.A. (1997) The effects of failure on children's ability to perform a musical test. *Psychology of Music*, 25: 18–34.

Pitts, S.E. (2009) Roots and routes in adult musical participation: investigating the impact of home and school on lifelong musical interest and involvement. *British Journal of Music Education*, 26(3): 241–256.

Ruddock, E. & Leong, S. (2005) 'I am unmusical': The verdict of self-judgement. *International Journal of Music Education*, 23: 9–22.

Sloboda, J.A. (2001) Emotion, functionality and the everyday experience of music: where does music education fit? *Music Education Research*, 3(2): 243–253.

Sloboda, J.A., Davidson, J.W., Howe, M.J.A. & Moore, D.G. (1996) The role of practice in the development of expert musical performance. *British Journal of Psychology*, 87: 287–309.

Sloboda, J.A., Wise, K. & Peretz, I. (2005) Quantifying tone deafness in the general population. *Annals of the New York Academy of Sciences*, 1060: 255–261.

Stålhammar, B. (2003) Music teaching and young people's own musical experience. *Music Education Research*, 5(1): 61–68.

Building Musical Bridges

Leonora Davies

Moving from primary to secondary school is a point at which young people's musical journeys can be significantly influenced, whether by design or default. This chapter examines some of the issues around transition and how they can affect young people's choices during the early stages of their musical journeys. It then describes some of the strategies that are being developed by the Musical Bridges project in order to improve the transition process. Further details of the Musical Bridges programme can be found at www.musicalbridges.org.uk.

Transition is not simply an academic transfer process; there are also emotional and social dimensions. (Harris & Davies, 2009: 122)

Our lives are shaped by a multiplicity of journeys both emotional and physical. We can all reflect on the various experiences that have influenced both our lives as a whole and our musical lives in particular. Transition from one phase of our lives to another is an important part of living and growing up and perhaps the most significant transitions we make are when we are young and travelling through our school lives.

Transition issues in context

Moves from one educational setting to another form a rite of passage for all children. When this is handled effectively it can provide beneficial landmarks as we grow up. (Paterson & Davies, 2005: 5)

In 1993, soon after the National Curriculum was introduced, Ofsted commented on issues that concerned them around the transfer of pupils between primary and secondary schools (Years 6 and 7). Recommendations were made by Ofsted in 1999 and yet again in 2009.

Effective partnerships between primary and secondary schools were extremely rare . . . virtually no information was being shared at the point at which pupils transferred to other schools except, at most, some information about which pupils learned musical instruments. (Ofsted, 2009: para 185)

For too many young people there is no clear or coherent pathway as they develop as musicians and many find the challenges and the barriers insurmountable and give up.

> Nothing is more de-motivating for pupils than the situation where at each point of transfer the teacher decides it is easier to 'start again'. (Glover & Young, 1999: 212)

Although this issue is recognized by pupils, parents, teachers, music leaders and government, our educational system still struggles with developing coherent and relevant pathways for pupils. We know that the reasons are many and various, for example:

- The large numbers of neighbouring primary schools transferring to any one secondary school
- The fact that, until recently, no one individual seemed to have specific responsibility for transition either within the local authority or within schools
- That it is only information about SATs results in the core subjects that is transferred to secondary schools

The Henley review and the government response highlight transition (both generically and musically) as an on-going issue which requires urgent attention.

> I welcome the work currently being undertaken by the Paul Hamlyn Foundation in funding the Musical Bridges programme with the aim of developing effective strategies for pupils moving from primary to secondary school. As this body of work develops, I believe it will provide valuable insights into this issue. (Henley, 2011: para 8.6)

The Musical Bridges programme

The Musical Bridges programme is funded by the Paul Hamlyn Foundation. It began in January 2010 and is scheduled to conclude in December 2012. Already it is providing valuable insights into the issues around transfer and transition and its emergent themes. The vision of Musical Bridges is that all 9–13-year-olds will experience a continuous and progressive musical experience which supports their personal, social and educational development.

During the first year of the Musical Bridges programme three core strands of activity have been established:

- A national evidence-gathering survey—Sound Tracks
- A pupil tracking longitudinal study—Changing Key
- A teacher professional development (CPD) strand

The Sound Tracks survey was launched in September 2010 in order to gather experiences about music-related transition as seen from the perspectives of primary and secondary school teachers, music services and music organizations. The results of the survey were published in a report in January 2011 which is available on the Musical Bridges website (www.musicalbridges.org.uk).

Changing Key is a research-based investigation that examines the role of music and music education in the development of 11–12-year-old children's psychology across the transfer period from primary to secondary. This is providing the 'pupil voice'. The final report will be published in September 2011 and can also be found on the Musical Bridges website.

The core objective of the CPD strand is to generate in-depth learning about effective pupil transition from KS2 to KS3 which enhances outcomes and strengthens musical progression between primary and secondary schools. This activity is currently taking place in Cornwall, Merton, Oldham and Wandsworth, working with music service colleagues and teachers from 28 schools. The schools represent clusters of primary and secondary schools. Practitioners have been involved in face to face activities as well as on-line materials. An immediate outcome of this phase will emerge in autumn 2011 as the teachers work together in team teaching situations in each others' schools on planned activities that they have developed.

In order to bring these three strands under the umbrella of a single framework we have used the 'Five Bridges of Transition' (Galton, Gray & Rudduck, 1999) as our key conceptual anchor point. It is generic in nature and does not have a subject focus. However, through our work on the programme, this is being developed into a musical self-assessment framework that is capable of monitoring the generic and music specific features of school transition.

The five bridges are:

Bridge 1   Administrative
Bridge 2   Social and Personal
Bridge 3   Curricular
Bridge 4   Pedagogic
Bridge 5   Managing Learning

For each bridge there are four suggested quality levels: introducing, establishing, extending and enhancing. This template was applied in the on-line Sound Tracks survey.

Emerging themes

The results of this initial work suggest that the most successful transition activities are where:

- KS2 and KS3 pupils actively engage in music-making together, preferably over a period of time, linking to the social and curricular support in Bridges 2 and 3
- There is recognizable pedagogic benefit for teachers from both key stages (Bridge 4)
- All potential partners build on shared understanding and a common purpose

One of the other emerging themes gathered through the original Sound Tracks questionnaire and Changing Key research suggests that the role of the Senior Leadership Team (SLT) is critically important. Productive cross-phase discourse or shared pedagogy *must* involve head teachers and SLTs in the arrangement and support for these activities and the staff involved. Any solutions to the challenges associated with musical transition need to speak generically to head teachers and SLTs so that links can be made between generic and musical issues (hence the use of the generic *Five Bridges*). Therefore, part of the Musical Bridges programme has involved an SLT strand of activity running parallel to the CPD strand. The first convergence of these two strands took place at three regional day sessions including presentations from SLT colleagues, Year 6 and Year 7 pupils as well as the involvement of parent governors. Extracts from a presentation made at one of those days by a head teacher of a primary school, auditing that school's current transition strategies, can be found on the webpage relating to this book on the NAME website at www.name.org.uk/publications.

Table 1 is from one of the areas taking part in the CPD strand. It is a developing document shared between music service colleagues and primary and secondary teachers, looking at ways of ensuring consistency of pedagogy between their two phases, and it shows clearly how generic statements are transformed into specific and relevant musical practice.

	Five Bridges generic statements	Current music service/school practice	Areas identified for development by schools and music service
Level 1: Introducing			
1.	An understanding of primary and secondary schools' approach to teaching and learning.	Primary and secondary teachers have an overview of the National Curriculum with regard to their own Key Stage and that which precedes/ follows on from it.	Many secondary school teachers do not have an understanding of *how* the KS1 & KS2 curriculum is taught.
2.	Advanced Skills Teachers provide outreach support to primary schools.	Specialist secondary music teachers visit feeder primary schools to work with children.	
Level 2: Establishing			
3.	Recognition and celebration of difference in teaching and learning: e.g. access to specialist teaching and resources.	Primary teachers and children have opportunities to visit secondary school and use specialist resources.	Secondary teachers should visit primary schools to see how teaching and learning takes place.
4.	Quality information to parents/carers about teaching and classroom practice.	Information to parents about what a music lesson 'looks like' ('sounds like'!) . . .	. . . in KS 1, 2 & 3.

5.	A common language for discussing teaching and learning: e.g. use of terms such as 'learning objectives', 'plenary', 'response partner' etc.	Common language: elements of music, composition, appraisal, performance, listening.	Different working groups within the secondary class.
6.	Active preparation of pupils to meet new ways of working.	Pupils attend 'taster' session at secondary school, or secondary music teacher visits primary school to introduce new ways of working . . .	. . . and for teachers to enhance their own teaching skills.
7.	Joint training programmes and professional development on teaching skills.	Joint training for Year 6 teachers, primary music co-ordinators and secondary music teachers.	
Level 3: Extending			
8.	Policies on teaching and learning shared across phases.	Music departments share schemes of work and teaching & learning/assessment policies with primary schools. Primary schools share the same docs with secondary schools.	
Level 4: Enhancing			
13.	Teacher exchange and secondment between primary and secondary schools.	Teacher exchange and secondment between primary and secondary schools.	This already happens with regards to Maths, English and Science. The success rate is very good in terms of children's learning experience etc. Extend to music.
14.	Schools in both phases evaluate and adapt their joint approach to transition, taking account of the pupils, teachers and parents.	Primary and secondary music colleagues work together to discuss musical learning, transition, students who play instruments, etc.	

Table 1: Bridge 4 Pedagogic

Passing on information

Another common theme relates to the passing on of information from one phase to another. Most music services now have in place systems for transferring records of pupils who continue with instrumental tuition. However, questionnaires which ask pupils 'Do you want to continue?' often invite negative responses. A more positive approach would be to assume that pupils *will* continue and for music services to provide such incentives as backing tracks so that pupils can practise and/or holiday courses or opportunities at the start the new term which encourage them to continue. However, this kind of information only deals with those pupils who have already received instrumental tuition. The Musical Bridges programme emphasizes the importance of inclusion and the need to recognize that *all* pupils will have musical experiences of one form or another to share and develop. The most effective way of transferring this kind of information is through the cross phase, face to face engagement of teachers and pupils as exemplified in the above framework.

During the first phase of our work, class teachers were encouraged to meet together to discuss possible plans for the forthcoming year and to develop ways of working and teaching together. Table 2 shows a chart developed in one primary/secondary cluster as an on-going working document.

Future developments

An online transition toolkit was developed following the publication of the *Sound Tracks* report. One of its main recommendations was that partners would probably need to engage in cross-sector collaboration if they were to successfully tackle the challenges of transfer and transition in their locality. The online toolkit is being structured in such a way as to facilitate effective partnership dialogue and collaboration.

The first step in devising this toolkit was to take the generic *Five Bridges* statements and 'translate' them into a bank of music relevant statements. We consulted with our 'community of engagement' to help us with this. An encouraging number of those who had responded to the initial survey had agreed to assist with further development and they were instrumental in helping us to produce a bank of 25 statements, grouped under five musical transition bridges.

We have now developed an online questionnaire that allows users to map their current transition activities (and the extent of their provision) against these criteria. Users fill in tick boxes based on current degree of activity across the range of strategies and activities.

The outcome of the questionnaire is a radar chart (see Figure 1), which provides a graphical 'audit' of the current strengths and weakness of provision across the Bridges. Radar charts can be used as a basis for mutual collaboration and support within a partnership or hub, leading to a coordinated action plan for improving provision for transition.

The Musical Bridges team, which includes colleagues from Trinity Guildhall and the OU, led by Programme Convenor, Adrian Chappell, is currently working on ways of extending the CPD programme beyond the current cohort of music services and potential hubs. Following a presentation at the FMS conference in June a number of services have expressed an interest and these possibilities are being actively pursued and developed. This work will develop through the autumn term of 2011 and throughout the year 2012.

Projects	Shared Department Aims	Pedagogy	Content/Teaching Strategies
PAST: Samba, Music/Dance/ Storytelling (i.e. all used as transition 'projects' in previous years) PRESENT: Musical Bridges! (i.e. using Musical Bridges principles and material)	• Develop brass playing and teaching. • Develop choral singing. • Teaching notation systems through engaging practical work — how can we best do this? • Establishing a sense of groove so students can perform different parts, on different instruments in secondary school?	• Same brass teacher? • Can we establish some common practice for teaching notation in a practical and engaging way? Does this matter? • Team teaching: 10 min section of lesson taken by primary teacher in secondary school and vice-versa. • Emphasis on the pedagogy explored throughout 'Musical Bridges': immersion, emphasis on collaborative, practical musical work, knowledge 'of' music and the importance of 'style' and 'feel'.	• Samba as 'bridging unit' from 6 into 7. • Where are students at the end of Yr 6 in terms of internalizing pulse/rhythm? Observations/video (does not have to be of samba!) • Whole class/teacher-led activities in secondary school should build on this by incorporating more complex rhythms and structures (signs, breaks) than currently used, singing and dynamics. These skills can then be exploited to a greater extent in the pupil-led, group composing task. • Team teaching idea: watch video of primary school Samba performance in secondary school as a way into a Samba composing task and a focus for discussion on what makes a good piece of Samba music.
FUTURE: **Massed Brass Band (performance Jun 2012)**, Choir? Steel Pans? Samba?	**Shared Resources** • Steel pans & samba instruments: better sets at the primary school than at the secondary school. • Guitars and ICT at the secondary school — none at the primary school.	• Secondary teacher will come to know pupils as musicians though engaging, practical work and conversations rather than a paper audit.	
Can we create a mini-hub involving other primary and secondary schools where links already established?	**Bringing additional schools into a mini-hub could enhance sharing of resources. Teachers are resources too!**	**How can we sustain this throughout other units?** **How can we emphasize the importance of style and feel in a unit like 'Programme Music'?**	**How can this be sustained throughout other units?**

Table 2: Musical Bridges cluster transition programme

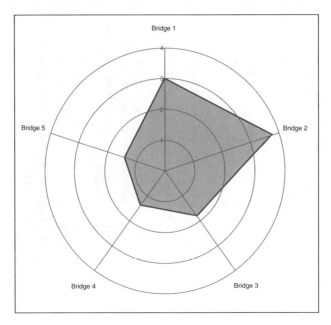

Figure 1: Radar chart used as an auditing tool

References

Galton, M., Gray, J. & Rudduck, J. (1999) *The impact of school transitions and transfers on pupil progress and attainment*. London: DfEE.

Glover, J. & Young, S. (1999) *Primary music: Later years*. London: Falmer Press.

Harris, P. & Davies, L. (2009) *Group music teaching in practice*. London: Faber.

Henley, D. (2011) *Music education in England*. London: Department for Education.

Paterson, A. & Davies, L. (eds.) (2005) *Rites of passage: Effective transition and curriculum continuity in music education*. Matlock: National Association of Music Educators.

Ofsted (2009) *Making more of music: An evaluation of music in schools 2005–08*. London: Ofsted.

Qualification and recognition for young musicians

Nick Beach

As suggested in the previous chapters, young people's musical pathways can be supported by the existence of frameworks which give them a sense of progression and purpose. Graded music exams have traditionally provided one such framework. In this chapter, Nick Beach considers the history of the graded music exam and looks at some of the ways in which examination boards are developing new forms of accreditation in response to current developments in music education.

In 1872 The Rev. Dr Bonavia Hunt set up the Church Choral Society and the College of Church Music, London, which were later to become Trinity College of Music. The purpose of these institutions was to improve the quality of music-making, particularly that performed in church, through raising the standard of teaching. Having established diploma qualifications for its students, Trinity was to break new ground as the first 'external' examination board in the world when it devised a theory syllabus and, shortly afterwards, graded assessments in practical subjects. These early exams were intended as a form of outreach, giving students a ladder by which they might ascend to the dizzy heights of the conservatoire. And a pretty good ladder it was, with Grade 8 equating to the sort of standard expected for music college entry. This outreach activity rapidly spread beyond England and by 1890 Trinity examiners were travelling on steamships to South Africa, Singapore, India, Sri Lanka, Australia and New Zealand for examining tours lasting many months. The other music colleges rapidly set up similar enterprises and soon the graded music exam had become the currency of musical development.

The graded music exam has been an extraordinarily robust affair and, whilst the exams have constantly evolved over the years in order to better reflect the needs of teachers and learners, there is still much in today's exams that those early examiners would recognize. And as a ladder of achievement they are still remarkably successful, although clearly, with the rising standards in music colleges over the years, they no longer provide the almost guaranteed path to the conservatoire that those early exams did. Perhaps the most successful feature of the graded exam, and an area which dogs many other assessment systems, is that they focus on 'stage not age'. We accept this as part of the music education furniture but actually it is rare for qualifications to completely ignore the age of the learner and focus on the levels of skills, knowledge and understanding demonstrated. For example, whilst convenient for a mass education system, suggesting that every child should take a GCSE at the same level and at the same age does not take account of the different ways in which children and young people learn, and the often seemingly disjointed way in which they progress. Viewed against this backdrop the graded exam, for all its venerable age, is quite radical.

According to Ofqual (n.d.), just over 400,000 candidates take a music graded exam every year in the UK. The DCMS survey of music participation amongst young people in England in 2009/10 suggested that around 70% of young people aged 11–15 play a musical instrument or sing (DCMS, 2010: 25). By extrapolating these figures we could assume that in any one year 5–10% of those playing a musical instrument or singing take an exam. On one level this is not surprising—many might take the view that young people learn music 'just for fun' or as a 'leisure activity'. But many children enjoy writing stories and do so 'just for fun' or as a 'leisure activity'—and we tend not to suggest that such children might not take GCSE English! We in the music education sector make great claims for the benefit of learning an instrument: not only the unique musical aspects but also, for example, creativity, literacy, numeracy, physical and social wellbeing. But if children and young people are engaging in an activity which is so critical for their development shouldn't many more of them be following recognized developmental and qualification pathways? Not to do so seems to suggest that musical activity is somehow less important than English, maths and science. For many young learners this is not the case.

Graded music exams clearly do not fulfil the same function they did in the late 19th century. In that period learning an instrument was restricted to wealthier families and group instrumental teaching was unheard of although, as Julie Evans (2011) notes, there were successful whole class programmes of violin teaching as early as the 1920s. Today access to instrumental learning is much broader, with first access programmes designed to give every child the chance to play music and sing. Many of these children do not have career aspirations in music so the historic function of the graded exam in preparing the candidate for music college has no relevance to them. However, in order to provide a focus and a framework for learning, alongside impartial and informed feedback on a performance, exams can be beneficial and valuable—as long as they are used in the right way.

This last point lies at the heart of many of the issues surrounding music graded exams, and is the root of most of the criticism of this system. Although we have earlier praised the 'stage not age' approach that graded exams take, this leaves them open to abuse. Teachers can push their pupils through grades at any speed they like. Sometimes overheard as teacher and Grade 4 pupil leave the exam venue are the words 'You can go and get the Grade 5 book now'. Following this developmental route it is possible to get from Grade 1 to Grade 8 having learned only 24 pieces! Too often, the comments by the examiner on the report form could actually be summarized as 'This candidate was entered for too high a grade'. Teachers and their pupils (and frequently their parents) are ambitious of course—and the temptation is always there to think that success in teaching, learning and musical development is purely measured by what grade a young musician has reached. It is not of course—the graded exam is only one way of measuring these things and the best teachers use a range of opportunities for assessment, within which external examinations take their place.

In recent years the examination boards have responded to changes in music education by starting to develop assessments which broaden both the range of instruments and musical styles represented, as well as the range of teaching styles and assessment methods (see Table 1).

Associated Board of the Royal Schools of Music (ABRSM)	**Music Medals**: teacher-led assessment for children in the early stages of learning an instrument **Jazz exams:** similar in structure to the graded exams and available for a range of instruments, including jazz ensembles
London College of Music (LCM)	**Leisure play:** performance-based exams without supporting tests
Rockschool	**Rock music exams:** following the traditional graded exam structure
Trinity College London	**Certificate exams:** performance-based exams without supporting tests **Music Tracks**: for first access and beginner groups (from 2012) **Rock and pop exams** (from 2012) **Arts Award:** portfolio qualifications covering all art forms.

Table 1: Range of available music assessments

Broadly, the new developments in music performance assessment could be grouped into three areas:

Qualifications and assessments for those in the early stages of playing a musical instrument. In this area the Music Medals from the ABRSM provide stepping stones for early learners through accredited certificates which are primarily assessed by the teacher. Trinity launches Music Tracks in 2012, which provides a progression route for children from having their first musical experience in whole classes through to entering for graded exams.

Qualifications focusing on different aspects of learning. Trinity's Certificate Exams and the Leisure Play exams from LCM focus on musical performance only, with no technical tests, aural tests, etc.

Qualifications in different musical styles. Rockschool run exams in rock music performance. In 2012 Trinity will be offering its own Rock and Pop syllabus.

On the one hand the range of new qualifications presents a rich range of options for teachers and learners, but on the other it is a complex mix which it is sometimes hard to find a way through. As a result many teachers either opt not to use any form of external assessment or to stick with what they know. This is a shame as, taken as a whole, the range of music qualification options available means that it is possible to meet the needs of a wide variety of learners, whatever their motivation for learning, their career aspirations or the musical style or genre in which they work. Table 2 below compares the standards required by the music qualifications available from ABRSM, LCM and Trinity College London.

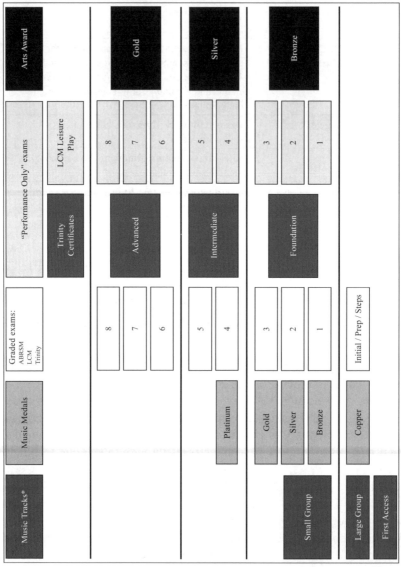

* Music Tracks launching Spring 2012

Table 2: Comparison of music qualifications

Although the various types of music qualification are represented here as columns, there is absolutely no reason why learners have to plough only one particular furrow. There are plenty of opportunities for plotting interesting development pathways across the columns that recognize that interests and priorities change. Indeed, this has the potential to create rich learning pathways that motivate and energize the learner.

We have talked a lot of awarding bodies in this chapter. Mention the words 'awarding body' or 'accreditation' in many artistic circles, particularly arts education circles, and you will feel the temperature drop. In many people's minds the function of an awarding body is to beat all the enjoyment, creativity, fun and real learning out of education! The real role of an awarding body is to certify the learning that has taken place. An effective awarding body does this through a deep understanding of the needs of learners and teachers. This supports the development of qualifications which are not artificial hoops to be jumped through but which provide a natural progression in the areas that effective teachers are covering anyway. At the same time useful qualifications need to be both valid (i.e. they assess what they set out to assess) and reliable (i.e. the same performance on different days with different examiners will receive the same mark).

The development of Arts Award presents an interesting illustration of the above. Arts Award began as an Arts Council England programme to encourage participation and leadership in the arts amongst young people. Interestingly it was young people who, during the early research, said loudly that they wanted an accredited qualification, not just a certificate. In the early days of Trinity's involvement as the awarding body for Arts Award there was some of the concern and distrust mentioned above. However throughout the entire development and roll-out process the development team remained true to the ethos and principles of Arts Award, with the young people and their creativity and leadership at the heart of the qualification. The fact that 13,000 arts leaders in England have now trained as Arts Award advisers is testament to the esteem in which this qualification is held.

The assessment model for Arts Award is one in which the adviser—who might be a teacher, youth leader or arts practitioner—plays the central role in assessment. There has been much discussion about the place of teacher assessment in qualifications but, where their assessment sits within appropriate moderation frameworks, it can offer both a reliable means of assessing progress and a valuable teaching tool for the assessor. The same approach underpins the Music Medals assessments from the ABRSM.

So what of the future? Where might music qualifications be heading and what might the chart above look like in 10 or 20 years time? Will graded exams still exist? It would be a brave person who made this sort of prediction, but the graded exam has had a knack of looking pretty contemporary at all stages in its development so it will probably be around for many years to come. The awarding bodies will continue to seek to offer a broad range of qualifications which support new forms of teaching and learning. In an increasingly multicultural environment they will find ways of ensuring that excellence in musical performance in all genres is properly recognized. But, most of all, perhaps a greater number of young people will be able to have their achievements recognized and celebrated through a credible qualification with real value and global currency.

References

Evans, J. (2011) How did we get here? The historical and social context of whole class instrumental and vocal teaching. In N. Beach, J. Evans & G. Spruce (eds.) *Making Music in the Primary School: Whole class instrumental and vocal teaching* (pp. 5–11). Abingdon: Routledge.

DCMS (Department for Culture, Media and Sport) (2010) Taking Part survey 2009–2010 Statistical worksheets: The Arts. www.culture.gov.uk/publications/7386.aspx [accessed 24.08.2011].

Ofqual (Office of Qualifications and Examinations Regulation) (n.d.) Vocational Qualifications Dataset: Regulated Qualifications Activity dataset—July 1988 to present. www.ofqual.gov.uk/downloads/category/171-vocational-qualifications-dataset [accessed 24.08.2011].

Becoming a professional musician: insights into the musical journeys of conservatoire students

Rosie Burt-Perkins

Some young people decide to embark upon a pathway as a professional musician and enrol on a course of higher education. This chapter looks at some of the aspects relating to the journeys of conservatoire students, both before and during their time at the conservatoire. It has been compiled from information and published papers from the Learning to Perform project, which ran at the Royal College of Music London from 2004 to 2008.

The *Learning to Perform* project, involving a three-year longitudinal study, investigated teaching and learning at the Royal College of Music London (RCM) in order to enhance understanding of musical expertise (Burt-Perkins, 2008). This chapter draws on papers arising from that and associated projects to provide brief snapshots of some of the aspects that contribute to students' musical journeys. Particular attention is paid to students' musical histories, their shift in attitudes during the first term at a conservatoire, and their changing identities and career aims as they develop into professional musicians.

Musical histories

Inevitably, an important part of conservatoire students' journeys involves their experiences prior to entering the conservatoire. While *Learning to Perform* did not track students prior to entry, the team asked 112 students to retrospectively chart the positive and negative experiences that they considered had 'influenced their development as musicians' (Burt & Mills, 2005: 2). Of the 717 listed experiences, only 50 were reported as negative. As the researchers point out, the pervasiveness of positive influences might reflect musical journeys that have included many 'successes' on the road towards the conservatoire. It might also be the case that students did not allow what could be perceived by others as a negative experience, such as failing a music exam, to have a detrimental effect, treating such events as challenges that led to personal and musical development rather than as off-putting setbacks.

Analysis of the most frequently cited experiences led to the construction of a 'typical' musical development history, which, in chronological order, comprised (with average age rounded up/down):

- Seeing siblings/parents making music (age 2)
- First lesson on any instrument (age 7)

- First lesson on current specialism (age 8)
- First performing opportunity (age 10)
- Other performing opportunity (age 13)
- First entrance to music institution—full/part time (age 14)
- Change of teacher (age 14)
- Other entrance to music institution—full/part time (age 16)

(see Burt & Mills, 2005: 2)

Of course, not all students cited each and all of these developmental experiences. Nonetheless, the kinds of experiences that students felt were influential to their development provide a glimpse into the sorts of events, opportunities and 'milestones' that characterize the musical journeys of pre-conservatoire students. Notably, these students' musical journeys appear often to begin with music in the home and are supported by a range of opportunities both to learn and to perform music.

Arriving at a conservatoire

Given that beginning at a music institution was cited twice in the 'typical' musical history, entry to a conservatoire can be seen as a major event in students' musical journeys and an important phase in their careers as professional musicians. As part of *Learning to Perform*, the team tracked the attitudes and experiences of students through their first term at a conservatoire (Burt & Mills, 2006), exploring how their hopes and fears shift and change during those transitionary months.

The researchers asked 20 students to complete a questionnaire before the beginning of their first term in order to collect data pertaining to what they looked forward to and were apprehensive about as musicians, as learners, and in areas other than music (*ibid.*: 53). A similar questionnaire half way through the first term and semi-structured interviews at the end of that term sought to elicit any changes in the original views, and a sub-group of students were also interviewed later in their first year and in their second year.

Much appears to change for musicians in their first term at the conservatoire, and Burt and Mills summarize this in terms of three 'pivot points' that can be seen to influence musicians' journeys: 'these points are events or achievements that can channel the students' experiences towards either a positive or negative outcome' (*ibid.*: 67). The authors propose three such points: students' first performance at the conservatoire, overcoming feelings of inadequacy and receiving useful feedback (*ibid.*: 68).

Given that performance is a central part of conservatoire life, Burt and Mills draw attention to the significance of the first time students perform to their new peers and teachers. Although a cause for apprehension among many students, 'the simple fact that they have passed through it allows them to move on and focus on other aspects of their development' (2006: 67). A successful performance and ensuing positive feedback from both tutors and peers played a significant part in reducing any fears about inadequacy and Burt and Mills therefore recommend that such an occasion should be experienced in the first term:

> This event is . . . highly important in that the consequences of not completing
> it in the first term may lead to continued and augmented fears of performing
> in front of esteemed peers, leading to a potentially damaging transition into
> undergraduate life. (*ibid.*: 67)

Indeed, many of the students — while looking forward to working alongside like-minded peers — found themselves feeling inadequate in comparison to others. Overcoming such feelings in order to progress at one's own pace became an important part of the learning journey, allowing young musicians to concentrate on their own development and their own progress. Linked with this, feedback relating to the first piece of written academic work — another 'first' causing apprehension — was also a pivot point in that autumn term, with positive feedback boosting confidence and more negative feedback seen as providing 'a learning experience' (*ibid.*: 61). Indeed, both formal and informal feedback emerges as a crucial part of these musicians' journeys.

Burt and Mills' work provides a glimpse into the complex, challenging and often highly personal nature of young musicians' journeys. Their enthusiasm for 'high quality teaching, opportunities, working in ensembles, studying alongside like-minded and talented peers as well as personal development' (*ibid.*: 69) runs alongside a realization that to become a professional musician will not be easy, often requiring them to step far outside of their comfort zone.

Changing identities and career aims

As the young musicians progressed through their conservatoire lives, the *Learning to Perform* team explored the developing identities, career aims and day-to-day practices of a group of 12 students (Burt, 2006). The students' descriptions of their identity fell into four categories: musician (n=7), student (n=4), teacher (n=2) and 'other' (in this case 'violinist' and 'performer'). Three students combined words to describe themselves as, respectively, 'musician/teacher', 'teacher/student' and 'musician and student' (*ibid.*: 7). However, even those who chose a single term with which to identify all described a wide range of musical and other activities. For example, a third-year student who identified herself as 'musician' detailed how:

> I try and do a couple of hours practice . . . an orchestral rehearsal . . . a
> rehearsal with a pianist. I will do quintet rehearsals and I have a faculty
> class and I will do gigs, occasionally freelance things that I get through
> college . . . I sing in a choir . . . I have my [instrumental] lessons . . . (Burt,
> 2006: 8)

The two students who explicitly included 'teacher' in their identity description demonstrate what seems to be an even fuller life:

> It [the work I do] is very varied which is why I love it. I have a job once
> a week teaching . . . I have two lectures in College . . . rehearsals, quartet
> rehearsals and quite often orchestra rehearsals . . . I have started doing a
> duet with one friend — one percussionist and sometimes we rehearse. My
> private lessons. As much practice as I can fit in . . . at the moment I am

> filling in for my friend's teaching because she is away . . . Sometimes I
> do gigs at the weekend. I have started doing Pilates once a week . . . and I
> enrolled in a gym . . . (*ibid.*: 8–9)

It is apparent from even this small group of students that there is a recognition of the breadth of activities needed to support varied musical roles. Indeed, as students progress through their conservatoire journey, they seem to also develop and broaden their identities (Burt-Perkins, 2008), learning what they want from a career in music, how to prepare themselves for this and—in some cases—redefining what they mean by 'success' as a musician.

Concurrently, shifts are also evident in students' career aims. A recurring theme to emerge from *Learning to Perform* was the students' 'unanimous hope to pursue a career in a music-related field' (Burt & Mills, 2006: 64). Although, as Burt and Mills point out, '[c]onsidering the nature of the degree course on which they were about to embark, this is not remarkable in the slightest', it does serve 'to illustrate the attitude that these young people have towards their chosen subject as a vocation' (*ibid.*: 64) even if the exact areas of career, or postgraduate study, are not quite as clear.

The authors report a 'divide' between those students who acknowledge the 'unpredictable and competitive nature of the profession', talking about their possible position after two years in 'flexible and uncertain' terms, with much use of the word 'hopefully', and, on the other hand, students who were already emphasizing their expected status in the profession even in their first term at college (Burt & Mills, 2006: 65). One apparently somewhat surprising finding was that students appeared to become 'more vague as to their career aims' during the early stages of their course, particularly as regarded performance careers, although this, together with composing, remained the majority expectation (*ibid.*: 66). However, such loss of definite intention may be partly due to an increased awareness both of reality and of other options, such as music therapy or music education. Teaching, however, was not often mentioned as a possible career by first-year students, with one person even remarking, 'I'm not at Music College to do that' (*ibid.*: 67)! This was possibly because students envisaged its needing an amount of experience such as that possessed by their own teachers—and thus too remote from their current stage—as it becomes a more popular option by the third year, with many students at that stage already having given instrumental lessons (see also above).

We know that 'portfolio' careers are now the norm for professional musicians, and Burt reports that '85% of 186 alumni who have left the conservatoire since 1994 combine performance with up to three other activities such as teaching, composing and music administration' (2006: 4). Indeed, the 12 students tracked by *Learning to Perform* not only detailed a range of identities but all anticipated working in more than one activity in their careers (which is why the total comes to more than 12):

- Element of career uncertainty (chosen by 7 students)
- Orchestral musician (5)
- Soloist (4)
- Finding enough work in music (4)
- Chamber music (3)

- Instrumental teacher (2)
- Making recordings (2)
- Education projects (1)
- Conducting (1)
- Not music (1)

(Burt, 2006: 6)

Within these activities, different students defined 'success' as being, variously, internationally recognized, well known, winning competitions, or being principals in orchestras (*ibid.*).

The amount of diversity in career aims differed, but students were unlikely to have only one professional activity in mind, especially as they neared the end of their conservatoire education. Indeed, one third-year student anticipated her career covering a range of musical roles and styles of music:

> I would like to be internationally recognized, whether as a soloist or as an orchestral musician . . . I would like to be the sort of person who wins all the competitions and goes around the world doing tours . . . I would like to have the sort of career my teacher has. He is a soloist here, and he does . . . recordings. He is principal of two London orchestras . . . he teaches [at the conservatoire] and . . . does film music . . . he just does all the sort of stuff that I really want to do—all these different areas. I don't want to be stuck in just one kind of area . . . (*ibid.*: 7)

This student's comments resonate with many other young musicians, reminding us that their musical journeys are, in many ways, only just beginning. Indeed, their time in higher education provides a stepping off point for their future careers in music, and we have seen that, at that stage,

> students . . . anticipate a diverse career (whether as a positive aspect of a professional life in music, or as an eventuality in such a career), that they have already begun to identify themselves holistically as 'musicians', and that they engage in activities that stretch beyond their specialism as part of their training. (*ibid.*: 11)

The journey towards professional musician is undoubtedly a challenging one, involving the development of a broad identity, of openness to diverse employment possibilities and the pursuit of both diverse and specialized musical activities. For the students involved in *Learning to Perform,* the journey emerges as musical but also personal, as their lives as musicians begin to take shape.

Acknowledgement

The *Learning to Perform: Instrumentalists and Instrumental Teachers* project was funded by the Economic and Social Research Council (ESRC) Teaching and Learning Research Programme in the UK. Project website: www.tlrp.org/learningtoperform.

References

Burt, R. (2006) *Students at a UK conservatoire of music: working towards a 'diverse employment portfolio'?* Paper presented at the ISME Commission for the Education of the Professional Musician 16th International Seminar, Hanoi, 10–14 July. www.tlrp.org/dspace/handle/123456789/556 [accessed 26.06.2011].

Burt, R. & Mills, J. (2005) *Charting the musical histories of students who aspire to become professional musicians.* Paper presented at the Performance Matters! Conference, Porto, Portugal, 14–17 September. www.tlrp.org/dspace/handle/123456789/388 [accessed 26.06.2011].

Burt, R. & Mills, J. (2006) Taking the plunge: The hopes and fears of students as they begin music college. *British Journal of Music Education* 23(1): 51–73.

Burt-Perkins, R. (2008) *Learning to Perform: Enhancing understanding of musical expertise.* Teaching and Learning Research Programme. www.tlrp.org/pub/documents/Mills%20RB%20 47%20FINAL.pdf [accessed 26.06.2011].

Progression routes in popular music

Simon Pitt

For young people who choose popular music, the pathways have often been less clearly defined than those in, say, classical music. However, the picture is changing, and there is now a range of accredited provision at school, college and university levels. Simon Pitt offers an overview of this provision which suggests that, perhaps in contradiction of received wisdom, there has been an increased demand for structured courses among prospective pop and rock musicians.

Introduction

Perhaps the most remarkable story of British music education of the last 20 years has been that of the rise of popular music. From virtually nothing in the late 1980s, the UK now boasts more than 70 university courses dedicated to some aspect of the industry along with thriving school and college programmes, accredited graded instrumental examinations and four major private teaching institutions. There is also a growing international network in the US and in Europe. The prospective student of popular music is now presented with an array of choices for progression pathways in music education. This chapter looks at how the sector has developed and examines the impact of pop in the classroom and on music education in general.

A little history

The British pop music industry of the last 50 years is one of the great cultural success stories of recent times. From 1963 onwards, British pop music played an increasingly pivotal role in the growth of western popular culture and today the figures are impressive. The UK pop music industry turns over £3 billion a year and more than 10% of global music has some form of British input in it whether on the production or the business side. The business is second only to banking and insurance in international earnings for the UK. Like it or not, pop pays and over 90% of musical activity in the UK, be it recordings or concerts, has popular music at its core (BPI, 2011; IFPI, 2011).

This rapid expansion of popular music education over the last two decades might strike the casual observer as somewhat counter-intuitive. After all, according to the stereotype, pop musicians shun formal teaching of all kinds and are only interested in gathering together in garages or other enclosed spaces to make as much unstructured and tuneless noise as possible, emerging from time to time to inflict this noise onto an unsuspecting public. Pop musicians are auto-didacts and their learning is properly located in an informal or even non-formal setting. Learning is a matter of trial and

autonomy

error and any success may in part be put down to happenstance and sheer good luck as much as musical training.

This picture of how pop musicians learn is seriously misleading. While most successful pop musicians remain reluctant to acknowledge any formal training they may have had, the function of 'universities of pop' prior to the rise of a formalized music education was nevertheless traditionally provided by art colleges. The roll of successful British pop musicians who can claim an art college education includes John Lennon, Pete Townshend, David Bowie, Brian Ferry, Malcolm McLaren (briefly), Ian Dury and Jarvis Cocker to name but a few. This is a tradition that dies hard even today with Ricky Wilson of the Kaiser Chiefs being one of the modern breed of 'pop art' pop stars. He waited so long for success to beckon he had enough time at Leeds Metropolitan University to gain a Masters in fine art.

Seen in this context, the growth of popular music education after 1990 is not such an anomaly. What fuelled the transition from a purely art school based education to something more specifically music focused has much to do with the emergence of some key private-public partnerships around the years 1989–1992; and it was the success of these partnerships that created the landscape of popular music education that we see operating today.

It is perhaps significant that most of the driving forces outside of the higher education system came from private initiatives that either tapped into latent demand for a more formalized education or were established to plug obvious gaps in the system as it then operated. The first private school of any significance, The Guitar Institute, was opened by Alan Limbrick (a graduate of the Musicians Institute in California) in Acton in 1989. This was quickly followed by the allied 'Tech Schools' (Basstech, Drumtech etc). The first grade validated examinations were offered by Rockschool and the Registry of Guitar Tutors in late 1992. The same year saw the foundation of Access to Music, offering courses in popular music.

The essentially private nature of these organizations is a testament to British inventiveness and drive as well as to the structural and cultural intransigence then existing in the school and college system. The grade examinations were created to allow students of popular instruments the opportunity to audition for the discretionary grants that were then available from local authorities for players who wanted to pursue further study at university. Only players who held a Grade 8 could do this at the time, so pop musicians were automatically excluded. The foundation of the Guitar Institute plugged an obvious gap in the market for students who wanted to make a serious study of pop instruments. Until then you either pored over the technique pages of *Guitarist* or *Rhythm* magazine or took pot luck on the quality of your local teacher.

Parallel to these private developments was a strand of public investment in popular music education that came in two parts. The first of these was the initial development of what later became the BTEC programme in popular music by Jim Joseph, a lecturer at Newcastle College. The second was the foundation of the first university courses in 'commercial music'. Pop music courses, such as those at West Lothian College and University College Salford, were already in existence, but the opening of the BA Commercial Music course at the University of Westminster in September 1993 was a significant development for a number of reasons. It was a wholly new university music department (i.e. it did not have to 'fit in' with either classical or jazz music) and it was based in London. It was set up with the 'art school model' in mind: that is, its main focus was on musical ideas rather than on technical ability on the instrument. The course catered for both songwriters/performers and music business professionals and in the first year of study required production and business students to learn each others' crafts. Business students had to understand what drives performance and recording ideas and to have a basic mastery of recording technology while the production students were required to understand that most art has economic consequences for the artist.

The impact of Westminster's degree courses cannot be underestimated. Its graduates, who include Tom Baxter, Kevin Mark Trail, The Feeling and Bridgette Amofah, found work in all avenues of the business as performing artists, producers, artist managers, record company executives, media composers, venue managers and booking agents. Its business graduates in particular swarmed all over the major and independent record labels, and still do. Part of the reason for the success of the course was the investment made by the University in its Harrow Campus (formerly Harrow College of Art, briefly attended by the late Malcolm McLaren) and the fact that students could integrate themselves into a single purpose-built campus that included many other aspects of the business, such as video, photography and fashion. It remains the largest popular music course in Europe.

Westminster's degree course was the beginning of a flood of new courses at higher education level from the 1990s onwards. There are now more than 70 universities in the UK offering courses with some form of music industry component. By 2011 there were also four private institutions: the Institute of Contemporary Music Performance (ICMP) in Kilburn, north London, the Academy of Contemporary Music (ACM) in Guildford, the Brighton Institute of Modern Music (BIMM), based in Brighton and Bristol, and the Tech Schools, based in Acton.

At further education level, there are more than 200 colleges offering some form of popular music courses accredited either by BTEC or Rockschool's Music Practitioner qualifications. Access to Music is now the largest delivery organization for popular music in England with nine big centres in major cities and a string of partner colleges. Its partner company, Armstrong Learning, based in Manchester, also operates the Music Industry Partnership (MIP) programme (formerly known as the New Deal for Musicians).

Outside these developments is a school which is unique in the recent history of popular music: the BRIT School, based in Selhurst, Croydon. To all intents and purposes an 'ordinary' secondary school, it is nevertheless one of the most celebrated performing arts and technology schools in the UK. Established in 1991 and part funded by the British Record Industry Trust (the organization that puts on the annual pop—and classical—awards each year), its alumni list reads like an honour roll of modern British pop: Adele, Amy Winehouse, Kate Nash, Katie Melua, Leona Lewis, Imogen Heap, Jessie J and individual members of bands such as The Feeling and The Kooks. Competition for places is fierce and it is one of the few schools which actually receives any attention in the music business with a ringing endorsement from Universal Music label boss, Lucian Grainge.

Progression routes from school to university: schools and colleges

A student who is seriously thinking of undertaking a career in popular music has a wide choice when it comes to what route to follow. It is likely that many students will be exposed to the possibility of learning a pop instrument at an early age and much of the demand for tuition at the ages of, say, 9–13 is as a direct result of the exposure that many students have to the wide range of media expressions of the genre, including iTunes and Spotify, MTV and particularly the talent shows Pop Idol, X-Factor and Britain's Got Talent, all of which are geared up to propel singers into the entertainment business in a very short time. Whatever the merits of these shows, they feed a demand for tuition in pop performance, particularly singing, at an early age.

The serious business of choosing which musical pathway to follow starts at secondary school and students are, at first, largely dependent on the musical focus of the school. Many schools offer learners a choice of music qualification at age 14 to suit all tastes, whether it be a more traditional music GCSE or its alternatives, such as BTEC, Music Practitioner, or NCFE. These types of qualifications are now accredited by Ofqual in England, Wales and Northern Ireland (Scotland has its own accreditation system) on the new Qualification and Credit Framework (QCF) as a series of units, rather than as qualifications per se, that each have a credit value. These units can, in theory, be built into specific qualifications (defined by credit value 'minima'), using 'rules of combination' common to all providers whose qualifications are deemed to be 'open' for such combination.

In practice, schools tend to pick a branded alternative to Music GCSE (which, along with all the other public exams, is not on the new framework). Depending on their size, these qualifications can be worth a number of 'points' equivalent to, or in excess of, a GCSE. Another development which will undoubtedly have a significant impact on the choice available to learners as they approach age 16 will be the take up of the English Baccalaureate which currently does not have a music component in it. This is likely to make the alternatives outlined above even more popular for those students wishing to make a serious study of music at school or college.

Schools which do not provide alternatives to a traditional GCSE Music course may allow their students to enrol on a pop course at a local college of further education at 14. Indeed, one of the significant trends in secondary education at present is the increased presence of FE colleges in the education of students at 14+. This is a trend kick-started earlier in the decade by the ill-fated Vocational Diplomas that saw students move around towns between schools and a central college hub. It is one likely to continue in future given the falling rolls of students at that age group and the more mixed models of delivery now applying in the sector.

Most students at QCF Level 2 (equivalent to GCSE A* –C) study a mixed curriculum regardless of the qualification they are enrolled on. This usually involves a range of units that include individual instrumental performance, music production, composition and maybe some business work either in event management or the basics of setting up a business. The same is true for Level 3 (equivalent to A-level) where the vocational approach is reinforced with a much broader choice of options that can include radio production, video, stage management and sound, DJ skills and a wider range of business units. The aim of such education is not only to prepare students for the world of work but also to broaden their horizons of what the music industry has to offer. Moreover, many of the 'jobs' that exist in the business are done by self-employed individuals or small teams of people: the industry thrives on entrepreneurs and trendsetters. As a consequence, the education is based on experiential learning with the aim of getting the students to produce portfolios of work. Much, if not all, of the assessment is internal, with external moderation used as a guarantor of quality, although, if the Wolf Report (DfE, 2011) has its way, this position could be about to change.

Universities

The pathway choices facing potential university entrants can strike students as bewildering. However, if they have come up through a vocational route they will usually find that they have a good chance of securing that essential audition that most higher education courses use as a means of choosing their student cohorts. One of the great advantages of the existing vocational courses over the traditional A-level is that much of the coursework mirrors what students will be learning at university and the best courses give students a head start in their search for a place. If students have a higher grade exam, such as a distinction at Grade 8 in an appropriate instrument, then so much the better, particularly if it is in bass, drums or keyboard.

Not all university courses are the same or have the same ethos, and not all follow the 'art school' model of the Westminster degree. Indeed, many courses offer students a kind of hybrid model with emphasis on both ideas and instrumental technique, and students and careers advisers should be aware of this when researching courses and making applications. This is certainly the case with those courses, such as the ones at Bath Spa University, or the BIMM course validated by Sussex University in Brighton, where not only is a hybrid model of delivery offered to students but the basis of study is a Foundation Degree with an option for an additional third year leading to a BA (Honours).

There are many factors that prospective students will weigh up when making their choices: the cost of higher education is such nowadays that choosing a local college is often the only viable option. Those with the ability to move outside their local area will need to evaluate two other major issues: location and the choice between public or private providers. The international music business is based in London. With only a few exceptions, all the major and most of the independent record labels are based in the capital, so for a performer or aspiring session musician being based in London is almost a *sine qua non*. This is not to discount the impact of courses at the Universities of Leeds, Salford or the Liverpool Institute of Performing Arts (LIPA), the University of the West of Scotland or the University of Glamorgan, but the pull of the business to London can be overwhelmingly strong.

Each college will have developed its own brand of uniqueness and one key factor is the ability of courses to help students to find employment in the industry that they want to work in. Many students are attracted to the idea of studying at one of the four private colleges mentioned above. All these institutions offer degrees accredited by significant universities, all focus on the development of instrumental skills as the core of what they do and all thrive on their ability to deliver students right into the heart of the industry through their founders' connections and influence.

More specialist courses cater for particular aspects of the business, particularly high end recording. The University of Surrey at Guildford is still the only university in the UK to offer students an accredited 'Tonmeister' (master of sound) course. The other university with a long-standing reputation for postgraduate degrees in recording is in York. Alternatively, students can go to the private sector and attend a course in recording offered by the School of Audio Engineering (SAE) which has locations all over the world. On the business side, Buckinghamshire New University offers a combined honours degree in business, consisting of a core curriculum followed by a subject specialism such as intellectual property law or marketing.

A small international network of popular music universities has started to develop over the last five years, allowing some students to study abroad as part of their degree. Two prominent European institutions are the Rock Akademie, which is part of Fontys University in the Netherlands, and the Pop Academy based in Mannheim, Germany. Some British students are still attracted to the idea of studying in the USA at one of the dedicated pop music schools such as Berkelee (based in Boston), the Musicians Institute (MI) in North Hollywood, or in the university system, such as UCLA (California—performance), the University of Miami (recording) or the University of New York (music business), to name but three.

Conclusions

There is no doubt that there has been considerable proliferation in all kinds of courses and education pathways relating to popular music. This has in part been fuelled by student demand and the competition for places, particularly at some universities, remains fierce. After 20 years of almost non-stop growth now is probably the time to reflect on the successes and failures of the education on offer to students. Does this kind of education actually deliver on its promises?

This is a tricky question to answer: it is one of the curious characteristics of popular music education that it is not particularly highly valued by the industry at which most of this education is aimed. Moreover, this is a business where, a few record and promotions companies aside, there are not many 'jobs' for students to go to: it is not like either banking or insurance. The most successful university courses are those which remind their students that it is they who are the 'agents of change' and they will find a niche for themselves if they prove they have the mix of skills necessary to survive. Many music business employees are not only self-employed but will probably work in more than one area of the business, and many performers will find that teaching takes up a significant proportion of their time and accounts for at least half their income. Rather oddly, this attitude is still prevalent on the business side where the emergence of industry-savvy graduates has actually been a wholesale success.

In schools and colleges, the impact of popular music on teaching and curriculum development over the last 20 years has been incalculable and we are witnessing a gradual shift towards a more pluralistic model of teaching and learning. For some, the holy grail of teaching is a holistic approach that sees both formal and informal musical traditions coming together in ensembles where orchestral players provide additional musical colour for electrified bands or pop players work with orchestral players on performances of classical repertoire.

This is a process which has yet to play out fully in the classroom (and elsewhere) but it will be interesting to see what the next 20 years will bring. There are a number of fundamental questions that still need to be addressed which are beyond the scope of this article, such as the quality and quantity of appropriately trained teachers who are not only competent in the popular side of the business but who can function within an environment of whole class teaching; the extent to which the classical and the contemporary either can (or want) to work together; and the development of a flexible and worthwhile curriculum and assessment framework that is functional and durable in a landscape where the only constant is one of change.

Further information about progression routes in popular music, including organizations and institutions referred to in the text, can be found on the webpage relating to this book on the NAME website at www.name.org/publications.

References

BPI (2011) *BPI Yearbook 2011*. London: British Phonographic Industry. www.bpi.co.uk [accessed 24.07.11].

DfE (2011) *Review of Vocational Education—The Wolf Report*. London: Department for Education.

IFPI (2011) *Recording Industry in Numbers 2011*. London: International Federation of Phonographic Industries. www.ifpi.org [accessed 24.07.11].

The myopic insect

Doug Bott and Jonathan Westrup

This chapter offers an attempted overview of musical pathways for children and young people with Special Educational Needs and Disabilities (SEND).

Music education for children and young people with special educational needs and disabilities (SEND) is a dynamic and exciting area of work. A thorough and well-informed overview of musical pathways in this sector would require the equivalent of an insect's compound eyesight, in order that we might perceive at a glance the kaleidoscope of different needs and abilities, as well as the many different approaches taken by specialist and non-specialist music educators. Instead we must admit that, like many others working with these children and young people, the outlook from which we write is likely to be considerably more myopic. Despite our best efforts we probably only understand limited areas of the kaleidoscope, and even then, may only be well informed about work taking place immediately in front of us.

So, before attempting this overview we must put our cards on the table, to give some indication as to the probable origins of our own professional myopia. Our educational work for Drake Music (DM Education) embraces a fairly wide variety of children and young people with SEND, but our core specialism lies in breaking down physically disabling barriers using Assistive Music Technology (AMT), through which we aim to broaden access to formal music education. DM Education began in 2007 as the Drake Music Curriculum Development Initiative, precisely because we were finding it difficult to obtain information on formal musical pathways for the students we work with. Consequently, a key part of DM Education is a series of new web pages on the Drake Music website (www.drakemusic.org/dm-education). These pages are a place to publicize and share information on all aspects of the SEND 'kaleidoscope' in relation to formal music education, the curriculum and accreditation, as well as providing a forum to share experiences and discuss issues.

In writing this overview it would also be desirable to reference lots of well researched facts and statistics that provide information on pathways open to differently disabled children and young people, with different musical interests, needs and aspirations, across all educational stages. However, such data is scarce and by no means comprehensive across a usefully wide range of SEND. For example, although Ofsted's *Making More of Music* report (Ofsted, 2009) made reference to improving music provision for those with least access, Ofsted have never yet carried out a report that focuses specifically on music provision for SEND students, although they do plan to include relevant figures as part of a three-year subject survey programme in music, due in 2012. Representatives of the Federation of Music Services (FMS) have told us that their records contain no specific data about participation by SEN students generally, only some anecdotal comments in the Wider Opportunities review. The Sounds of Intent research conducted jointly by the Institute of Education, Roehampton University, and the RNIB is providing extremely valuable information relating to children and young people with learning difficulties in the areas of complex needs, profound and multiple learning difficulties (PMLD) and Autistic Spectrum Disorder (ASD), culminating in the excellent Sounds of Intent framework and website (www. soundsofintent.org). However, this is by no means representative of the entire 'kaleidoscope'; for example, it is not yet clear how relevant Sounds of Intent will be to those children and young people with SEND who face significant barriers to music, but are functioning beyond the stage of early musical development that is Sounds of Intent's clearly defined remit.

And so, bearing all this in mind, we come at last to our attempted overview of musical pathways for children and young people with SEND.

First, let's get **music therapy** out of the way, because even in 2011 there remains a stubbornly persistent assumption that musical activity for many children and young people with SEND is unlikely to be for any purpose other than therapeutic. Music therapy is an extremely valuable musical pathway for those who need it, as are physiotherapy or aromatherapy for their respective purposes. But music therapy is not music education; it is a process in which 'music-making forms the basis for communication' in a relationship between therapist and client where 'the therapist does not teach the client to sing or play an instrument' but instead 'aims to facilitate positive changes in behaviour and emotional well-being' (APMT, 2008). Music therapy does not seek to equip children and young people with musical skills and understanding beyond those necessary within a clinical context, where music is the therapeutic conduit, rather than the ultimate goal.

Informal musical activity provides important musical pathways for many children & young people with SEND. Specialist organizations focusing on different areas of the SEND kaleidoscope such as Music and The Deaf, Sound About and Drake Music provide a variety of informal musical activities. There are also many community and non-statutory organizations which run accessible, informal music education projects as part of their wider remit, such as More Music in Morecambe, The Music Pool in Hereford and Plymouth Music Zone. But the availability of such provision is a postcode lottery, depending on whether relevant groups operate in your area. These organizations also rely on fluctuating funding streams that are not always well suited to delivering consistent musical pathways over sustained periods.

Formal music education in school as part of the National Curriculum is the main interface with music-making for many children and young people with SEND, and is therefore a crucial musical pathway. For this reason alone it is important that music remains part of the National Curriculum. It is also the area to which we will be devoting the majority our attention in this overview.

There are relatively few specialist music teachers in special education in comparison with mainstream schools, so quality provision is still patchy and reliant to an extent on non-specialist school staff, those Music Services that have made SEND a priority, and the community or non-statutory music organizations mentioned above. As part of DM Education we are beginning to work with teacher training institutions to raise awareness of accessible music-making, in the hope that the number of music teachers who are motivated and trained to work with children and young people with SEND will increase over time.

In the primary phase, a number of musical pathways have opened up over the last two years in relation to singing, thanks to Sing Up's 'Beyond The Mainstream' work. Accessible singing resources have been created for the Sing Up Song Bank website by organizations such as The Makaton Charity, Music and The Deaf, Drake Music and Prima Vista, supported by a nationwide training programme. Other accessible resources include the *Zoobiedoo* song book (Batson *et. al.*, 2010), which is full of multi-sensory music and singing activities, and the *Crackers Maracas* resource pack (Hunt, 2011) for singing with children on the autistic spectrum.

Moving on to Key Stages 3 & 4, some exam boards and awarding bodies provide flexible music courses appropriate for young people with a range of SEND at different academic levels. ASDAN (the Award Scheme Development and Accreditation Network) provide courses incorporating music, such as Expressive Arts, Towards Independence and even Literacy and Numeracy in Everyday Life. The AQA (Assessment and Qualifications Alliance) Unit Award Scheme includes scores of ready-made music awards and a framework that enables music educators to create their own awards, which can then be accredited by AQA. The Trinity Guildhall Arts Award provides a popular pathway to accreditation in music that is accessible to many young people with SEND.

While these courses provide a flexible framework for study and a means to accreditation, they do not in themselves open up musical pathways for children and young people who face more significant barriers to music. They are useful in terms of outlining the *what*, but are not designed to provide teachers with much in terms of the *how*. Adaptable schemes of work and carefully worded learning outcomes cannot in themselves make these courses accessible to young people who, for example, may rely on Assistive Music Technology or other specialized means of access. It still remains for music educators to translate the course materials into tangible resources and activities that are accessible to a variety of differently disabled young people. This can be an extremely challenging prospect for teachers who are pushed for time, working within tight budgets and who may lack the necessary technical expertise.

As part of DM Education we are promoting the importance of creating and sharing accessible software resources, which not only make musical pathways accessible to students, but also provide a course framework for teachers. Ultimately, we hope that such resources will make it possible for more teachers to provide for children and young people with SEND. We are creating the *Music Motivator* course in partnership with Barrs Court Special School & College in Hereford. *Music Motivator* provides a structured framework of music activities and resources appropriate for young with learning difficulties at KS3/4, whose progress is being assessed against 'P'-levels. We are also piloting accessible resources for BTEC Performing Arts and Music in partnership with Claremont School in Bristol. We plan to disseminate both the *Music Motivator* and BTEC resources and course materials once the pilots are complete. We have also created our own *Introduction to Music* course, accredited by OCNSWR

(Open College Network South West Region) at Entry Level, Level 1 and Level 2. The course consists of four units, combining practical performing and composing activities with learning and assessment resources for Clicker 5 software, which is physically accessible to almost any student. *Introduction to Music* is now available from Drake Music and is free to any Open College Network centre in England, Wales or Northern Ireland.

In theory, all academic music exams, including GCSE and A-level, are accessible to any student working at the appropriate academic level, as required by the Special Educational Needs and Disability Act (SENDA). But few pathways are tried and tested across a broad spectrum of SEND and the lack of precedents means that it is not often clear how access is actually to be afforded. In our experience and based on anecdotal evidence from other music educators, the major exam boards can be extremely reluctant to discuss potential special arrangements in advance of commencing a course, which makes it almost impossible to timetable students, staff and resources appropriately. WJEC (Welsh Joint Education Committee) are one of the more approachable awarding bodies providing GCSE as well as Entry Level qualifications in music, though none come with ready-made accessible resources of the type we have developed for the Drake Music *Introduction to Music* course.

For assessing **Musical Performance** there are a number of musical pathways that, if necessary, can provide an alternative to conventional music grade exams. The London College of Music (LCM) provides *Leisure Play*, which can accommodate performance on almost any instrument. Worcester Snoezelen centre have successfully entered a number of disabled people for LCM exams. One is a profoundly deaf person on the autistic spectrum who played Soundbeam in conjunction with vibroacoustics (allowing her to feel sound) and audio-visuals (allowing her to 'see' sound). Another is a young blind child who, as described by one of the Music Leaders at Snoezelen, 'has a joyful and innate sense of rhythm ahead of her years. She listened and responded to various rhythms and musical styles, and when prompted demonstrated her ability to perform music asked of her'. Similarly, ABRSM provide opportunities for Performance Assessment, and Trinity College run Music Certificate Exams that are more adaptable than their Music Grade Exams, permitting students to choose their own repertoire. In 2004, disabled musician Rhona Smith achieved a Trinity Guildhall Music Certificate using E-Scape Assistive Music Technology.

It's inevitable that on reading this overview, many of you will be keen to point out musical pathways we've failed to mention, or to put us right on things you think we've got wrong. If so, we would urge you to go to www.drakemusic.org/dm-education and create an account — it only takes two minutes. You can then share your knowledge of musical resources and courses that are accessible to children and young people with SEND, as well as your experiences in this area. You will also find much more detail and be able to comment on the musical pathways mentioned in this article. It is our sincere hope that through sharing information we can collectively move away from 'professional myopia' towards a more compound and coherent overview of accessible musical pathways across the SEND kaleidoscope.

References

APMT (2008) *What is music therapy?* Association of Professional Music Therapists/British Association for Music Therapy. www.apmt.org [accessed 24.07.11].

Batson, A., Ballard, B. & Grew, N. (2010) *Zoobiedoo: a multi-sensory music, singing and activity resource.* Plymouth: Plymouth Music Zone Publishing.

Hunt, C. (2011) *Crackers maracas: a singing resource for children and young people on the autism spectrum.* Gateshead: The Sage Gateshead.

Ofsted (2009) *Making more of music: an evaluation of music in schools 2005–2008.* London: Ofsted.

How community musicians learn

Kathryn Deane

Much musical activity takes place outside the formal education sector, facilitated by musicians who have often learned their skills in an informal way. This chapter looks at the skills and understandings needed by community musicians and the ways in which they can be developed through a combination of experience and qualifications.

Let me tell you about Sam. Sam is not her real name. Sam is not even an individual person: she's a composite from surveys undertaken over the years by Sound Sense (the UK professional association for community musicians). These surveys have looked at who community musicians are and what and how they learn (see *Surveying community musicians* box below). Sam was immersed in music from an early age — festivals, home singalongs, sackfuls of tapes — and can trace formative musical memories back to the age of five or even earlier: 'My mum used to play and teach piano from home when I was very young. I remember us having sing-a-long nursery rhyme sessions, so music was a part of my life since I was very young. I remember realizing how important the piano was to my mum when we wheeled it down the road to a friend's house at midnight.'

Sam loved her primary school music activities, but at secondary school music 'became bound by rules, a fearful thing, getting things wrong, then getting something else wrong, then something else wrong again. Music, it seemed, was only for the gifted kids, and I was never one of those.' She didn't settle down musically until she found both an instrument and a teacher she could get on with. She didn't go to music college, but mucked around in bands, and learned the important difference between being good at playing an instrument and being a good player of an instrument with other people.

For her day job, Sam became a youth worker. And more and more she realized the transformational effect music was having on the young people she worked with, and more and more she tried to weave music into her activities. Until the day came when she realized she wasn't a youth worker doing a bit of music, but a musician helping to develop young people through music. Though she didn't know the term 'community music' then, that's what she was practising: music-making which, in the words of Sound Sense's long-standing description:

- Involves musicians from any musical discipline working with people to enable them to develop active and creative participation in music
- Is concerned with putting equal opportunities into practice
- Happens in all types of community, however defined, where it reflects the context in which it takes place.

Lightbulb moments helped her development as a community musician. Whether as a young person or later, musical milestones for Sam tended to be connected to people: 'I wasn't really ready to play in a brass band, and my first practice on third cornet was a pretty terrifying experience. However, I loved the music and the sense of community, with different generations working together.' Or to confidence: 'In a smoky, (pre-ban) pub, to about 11 people, I found the thrill of singing and an ounce of confidence to consider myself capable of impacting others with my music.'

She found a short course which made her realize several things: that what she had been doing in her music work had a name (several names, in fact, of which community music was just one); that she could learn how to do it better; that she could make some sort of a living out of doing it; and that her passion for this type of work was shared and understood by others. Sam is now a fully-fledged community musician. Her musical pathway has been largely experiential: learning through working, learning after working, topping up her knowledge with specific activities when she's needed to.

Indeed, community musicians—whether the composite Sam above or the individual examples described below—seem hungry to learn. They learn by doing and from more experienced practitioners. They learn from their mistakes. They learn about social and political contexts, and how they apply to their work. They find role models and, well, according to Oliver, they pretty much stalk them. They go on courses—Oliver again: 'I find the time. Scrape the money. Blag funding from anyone I am working for. Breathe it in, digest the lot, let it expand my knowledge and root my philosophy.' They are living examples of Donald Schön's learning organization (1983/1991) and David Kolb's reflective practice learning cycle (1984): 'I have learned the most from observing other teachers and community musicians, both as part of my own development and throughout my career,' says Liz. 'I love the opportunity to reflect openly and honestly with the people whom I've worked with or employed and I would say that this honest reflection is a key part of the role of a community musician.'

In a survey carried out by Sound Sense in 1999 we found that community musicians were younger, poorer, with lower-level formal qualifications, twice as likely to be disabled, twice as likely to be from a black or minority ethnic background as other forms of music educator. In all of this they mirror their participants, so it may be no coincidence that the way they work with participants—experientially—is the same way that many of them learn.

From another survey, we started to understand more about this identification of practitioner with participant:

> Community music seems to me to be distinct from both teaching and therapy. It's important to protect the informal routes into music-making through self-taught skills, learning with peers, informal mentoring, and all the potential for rebel music-making in just picking up an instrument and seeing what you can do with it. . . . What happened to the idea of playing music for the joy it brings, or because it comes from within and you really have to do it? It follows from this that we need a range of people working in community music, and there must be room for those of us who have

become musicians informally but have loads of experience at all levels of
music-making that we can pass on.

Experientialism may also be why some of the famous formal courses and qualifications
in community music—such as the certificate in workshop skills from Goldsmiths
University of London—have an intake of students who are already proficient
community musicians: you learn *how* to do your job on the job; you then later learn
to understand *why* you're doing it in the way you're doing it with more formal
training.

But this isn't the only learning pathway for a community musician, of course:
another Sam (that is actually his real name) went to Huddersfield University, learning
improvisation and contemporary music on his performance degree; Liz went to City
University 'because I didn't want to be a performer and I loved the diversity offered
in the course—modules such as improvisation and cognition, ethnomusicology, sound
recording, electroacoustic music, Indian music, acoustics, Arabic music, composition
really inspired me.'

And young people are not the only client group community musicians work with;
in a survey of the Sound Sense constituency in 2006, we found that they were indeed
very likely to work in formal education settings—not only in schools and pre-school,
but significantly with adult education as well. But they were even more likely to work
in non-formal community settings—again, not only with young people but nearly as
much with older people, and with a significant emphasis on working with disabled
people; and again, across a wide range of settings.

So the musical pathways for a community musician are convoluted, multiple and
not always clearly signposted. You might start out as a participant in a project before
realizing that what it was achieving for you was something you could help others to
achieve. Often, people say they became a community musician 'by accident'. Liz
cites her brass band work as a true community music project and adds, 'I love music
and, without sounding cheesy, wanted to do something where I was helping people,
so this area seemed ideal for me.' Sam compared his formal teaching activities with
his attempts at community music 'and after a couple of years knew that I enjoyed
community music projects much more than teaching singing.'

All this experientialism and informal apprenticeships does not mean that community
musicians are allergic to gaining qualifications. Our surveys looking at community
musicians' attitudes to qualifications turn up a huge variety of qualifications being
claimed, ranging from psychology and social work to linguistics degrees and an HND
in mentoring; and taking in most forms of music-making and teaching qualifications at
all sorts of levels—not only the PGCEs, but also the PTLLS and DTLLS (Preparing
for/Diploma in Teaching in the Lifelong Learning Sector). Almost everyone responding
had at least something (though some very established community musicians had no
formal qualifications), and whatever it was, as learning it had invariably proved helpful
to them.

But as a recognized qualification when looking for a job? Much less important: only
around a quarter reckoned their qualifications had been required for a particular job. 'I
find people are actually more interested in my attitude to the work being offered, the

experience I have and whether I have been CRB checked. They also want to know how much I charge because of their (often limited) budgets' was a typical response. Oliver has a philosophical view: 'What we believe leads what we think, which leads what we say and do, which dictates our practice. So, don't take any course for a qualification, take them to deepen what you believe about how music impacts the heart and soul.'

Liz takes a more pragmatic line:

> I think that any qualification giving practical experience of working creatively with people of all ages, abilities and different instrumentations is essential for community musicians, together with excellent communication and reflection skills, the ability to think outside the box and on your feet.

She also boiled down the *qualities* — rather than qualifications — a community musician needs into a list few would disagree with:

- A good ear and a sound theoretical understanding of many different instruments/keys, etc, so that anyone attending a session can be engaged. Confidence in using your voice. A creative and collaborative approach to composition. The ability to work with people of all musical experiences and traditions, and the ability to work with different types of learner, being able to present musical ideas in different ways.
- Excellent communication and listening skills. A personality (dynamic or calming as appropriate) that pulls people in and engages them. The ability to work in a non-judgmental way, sometimes with some quite challenging people and situations. The ability to find a starting point to engage someone where they are, but then to extend their experiences. The ability to work with others (other musicians, other professionals) and give and take constructive reflection.
- The ability to reflect openly and honestly about things that worked and didn't work. Good planning skills and excellent differentiation ideas, while being prepared to trash plans if needed.

Because for a community musician it's all about *engaging with people* — wherever they are and whoever they are. Even when we ask about practitioners' musical skills we're likely to get a people-focused answer: 'Able to get people who are not confident to believe in their voices and create great sounds.' Other answers that crop up regularly are around the importance of being able to improvise and, says Simon, 'My ability to play a wide variety of instruments (not particularly well but well enough) and find my way around the vast majority of music technology.'

We built all of these qualities of community musicians into the music education code of practice, which invites music practitioners to sign up to six core principles of their work. By adopting the code, a community musician makes good practice commitments, to:

- *Being well prepared and organized* including understanding the context of the project and what success would mean for participants

- *Being safe and responsible* for insurance, risk assessments, vulnerable adult protection and the like
- *Having appropriate musical skills* 'sufficient to undertake the work I am doing'
- *Working well with people* valuing and respecting participants, sensitive and responsive to both group and individual dynamics
- *Evaluating and reflecting on their work* monitoring, evaluation and feedback
- *Committing to professional development* improving and updating skills, knowledge and creativity

This is a good code to live by, full of the people skills community musicians say they need and have. Over the last 25 years community musicians have got better at being both music workers and community development workers. They understand the import of their work better, and they actively seek specific outcomes in their projects. In time we hope (see *ArtWorks* box below) that it will lead, on its own pathway, through occupational standards; and be the basis for informing any necessary future qualifications.

The community musicians we asked see their future pathways in even more learning ('I am also considering looking at becoming a music therapist in some form, using my skill set to help under-fives from in-care backgrounds'); more growing ('I'm in the process of scaling the organization that I've started'); and more supporting other practitioners and participants ('Creating opportunities for people to emerge from within the groups to continue the process'). But, above all, more making music with people — 'because that's the fun bit, right?'

References

Kolb, D. (1984) *Experiential learning: Experience as the source of learning and development.* Englewood Cliffs, New Jersey: Prentice Hall.

Schön, D. (1983, rev. 1991) *The reflective practitioner. How professionals think in action.* London: Temple Smith.

Surveying community musicians

How does Sound Sense know what community musicians want and need? We talk to them, both informally and formally. Key surveys over time, telling very similar tales, have included:

1999 *The music industry: skills and training needs in the 21st century* by Metier (the forerunner of CCSkills).

2006 *Sound Sense constituency analysis* A survey of our members and others in our constituency. Community musicians were very eclectic in their music, and very broad in the range of client groups they work with.

2007 *Qualifications survey* Members' attitudes to qualifications.

2011 *Musical pathways* Vox pops from Sound Sense board members describing their professional musical journeys.

Thanks to all the Sound Sense members who have helped us with surveys over the years.

ArtWorks

ArtWorks: Developing practice in participatory settings is a new initiative to support the continuing professional development of artists working in participatory settings from 2011 to 2014, and being delivered by five 'pathfinders'. Sound Sense is part of the Navigator pathfinder, working alongside colleagues in dance, literature, visual arts and gallery education negotiating access to, quality of, and understanding around training and professional development for artists working in participatory settings.

The richness of the Navigator partnership gives us the opportunity to interrogate practice in two dimensions: by setting and by art form. A question for the first dimension might be about whether there is a core of practice which is common across client settings: is the quality way you work with looked-after children, say, inherently different from the quality way you'd work with older people with dementia, or is there a common core of practice? A question for the second dimension might be around pre-professional training: in some art forms practitioners might be expected to be graduates before they even think about becoming community artists; in music the issue is much more polarized, stereotypically by genre: western classically-trained community musicians are very likely to have a first degree, while rock and urban musicians typically won't. What do those sorts of differences tell us about place of higher education in the development of community artists?

ArtWorks is a Paul Hamlyn Foundation special initiative with support and funding from the Arts and Humanities Research Council, Creativity Culture & Education (supported by Arts Council England) and the Cultural Leadership Programme.

ArtWorks: www.artworksphf.org.uk

Navigator: www.soundsense.org/metadot/index.pl?id=26493&isa=Category&op=show

---

The music education code of practice for music practitioners can be accessed via the Sound Sense website: www.soundsense.org.

A version of this article appeared in Sounding Board *2011 issue 2.*

Section 2

Surveying the Field

Learning all the time:
findings from the **NAME** questionnaire

Chris Harrison & Lis McCullough

To complement the other chapters in this book, a questionnaire was accessible on the NAME website between 27 May 2011 and 4 June 2011 with an invitation for members and non-members to describe their musical experiences and how they developed their expertise as musicians and/or music teachers. The purpose of the survey was to explore different musical pathways that people have taken, and identify any particular issues, themes or trends that could be drawn from their experiences.

The questionnaire and associated information are on the NAME website on the page relating to this book (see www.name.org.uk/publications), but the main questions were as in Figure 1.

---

1. What first interested you in music as a child?
2. Can you describe any early formative musical experiences?
3. What do you think were the most important 'milestones' in your musical development, and why?
4. Who have you learnt most from, and why?
5. What do you consider to be your most important musical skills, and how did you learn them?
6. What factors have influenced your choice of music-making activities?
7. When and why did you decide to become involved in music education?
8. What do you consider to be your most effective teaching skills and how did you develop them?
9. How would you like your 'pathway' to continue? Where do you see yourself, musically, in five years' time?
10. Is there anything else you would like to add in relation to your own experience?

Figure 1: Musical pathways questionnaire

Response

There was a very positive response to an initial invitation to complete the questionnaire, so that a follow up email from the NAME administrator on 24 June could report that 'a lot of people have told us they've really enjoyed doing it'. Several people made comments within their answers implying the pleasure the memories gave them, for example: 'Even thinking about [my parents] playing the piano and guitar makes me smile as I write this now'.

85 completed responses were received either online or via email attachment by the time the survey closed. The percentages in the following sections have been rounded

up/down for convenience and ease of reading. As with all such surveys, it should be remembered that findings are based on what the respondents wrote at the time and that, for example, some questions may have been omitted, or have been differently interpreted, by various respondents. There is an abundance of fascinating information in these responses and for reasons of space and time the following report highlights only the most striking findings from each question. There was some overlap between questions/answers, but the quotes given come from the specific question where they were included.

Respondents

61% could be identified as female, 25% were male and the other 14% were anonymous. Ages appeared to range from higher education student through to post-retirement.

In a section asking about **Current employment and/or main musical involvement** there was no indication of occupation from about 13% of respondents. Of those who *did* give some information about their current or previous career, although there was some overlap:

- Over 80% were, or had been, involved in some aspect of music education either in a salaried or freelance basis (schools, music services, advisory, ITE . . .)
- Over 10% were involved professionally with music other than in specifically *educational* fields (instrumentalists, music research, journalism, administration, charity . . .)
- 6% were involved in areas of education other than music (taught other subjects, consultants . . .) and
- The remainder worked neither in music or education (nursing, social services, customer services . . .).

There was no question about country of origin, and most people apparently, and understandably, came from the UK. However, one respondent worked in kindergartens in Mexico; another came from Korea, albeit was currently a PGCE student in the UK; and the following countries were also mentioned as having featured in individuals' journeys: Greece, Australia, Bali, Singapore, Argentina and S. Africa.

When it came to other **musical involvement**, about 30% mentioned taking part in singing-related activities (community choirs, festivals, a cappella, folk groups), with an overlapping 30% playing instruments (piano, violin, viola, saxophone, guitar, cello, double bass, cornet, trumpet, recorder, flute, clarinet, Korean instruments, drums, steel pans, as well as a *'Bellringer—does this count as music?'*). Styles and genres ranged across western classical, orchestral, chamber, folk, jazz, big band, brass bands, samba, church, gospel, funk, musical theatre and opera. Conducting, composing/arranging and listening were also mentioned as forms of musical participation.

The following sections consider the main findings from each question as numbered in the questionnaire.

1. What first interested you in music as a child?

70% cited family as early influences—mostly, as in the following examples, directly:

> 'There was a family culture of respect for music, attending concerts and valuing musical experiences highly.'

> '"Musical" family (so it seemed normal).'

> 'There was always music in our house.'

> 'My mum is a professional musician/teacher.'

> 'My father played the violin and I wanted "to play the violin like Daddy".'

> 'I . . . sang nursery rhymes with my mother, and she tells me I frequently made up my own songs.'

> 'Listening to my parents' records—Bach, Caribbean music, Ralph Harris stick in my mind.'

> 'I was interested at a very early age. My grandmother gave me a recorder and book for my birthday when I was under 5.'

But there was also less directly 'musical' but equally practical support, as in the following example:

> 'Came from a 'non' musical family and music was not played at home. I started learning an instrument when I was 11 after I went to call for a friend . . . and she was practising the saxophone . . . I had never seen a saxophone before . . . but was immediately drawn to it and rushed home and asked my parents for one. They hired one for me for 6 months as they thought it would be a fad and the rest is history.'

Instruments and what could be done with them also featured:

> 'Being able to play a song I knew on the piano.'

> 'My fascination with string instruments came from watching an episode of Pebble Mill with a string quartet when I was 6 or 7 which made me want to play the violin.'

While several responses related to the attraction of music itself: 'Attractive sounds', 'The tingle factor.'

There was frequent mention of schools and teachers (class and instrumental) and the opportunities they offered for structured and group music-making:

> 'Inspirational Music teacher at primary school'

'I really loved my lessons, performing in the primary school orchestra, playing in the recorder group and singing in the choir.'

' . . . my interest really began when it was compulsory for all first year senior school students to study an orchestral instrument for a year. I applied to play flute but the school did not have enough flutes so I was allocated a cello!'

Live performances (and see the next section) were also picked out as having had an influential effect: 'My parents took me to live musical performance at a very early age, centred around Gilbert and Sullivan . . . '

2. Can you describe any early formative musical experiences?

It is not surprising that family members and teachers were again strongly represented in this section. However, the most frequently cited formative experiences related to live music, with 45% of respondents describing attending or performing in concerts, and many people remembering specific pieces.

It seems to have been big—often classical music—concerts that had the most profound effect on the respondents when audience members:

'I can remember the first time I saw a professional orchestra like it was yesterday. I was in awe of the wall of sound that I was confronted with.'

'Being taken to a Teddy bears concert at the Barbican.'

'Going to my first 'classical' concert (one of the Ernest Read ones I think) arranged by [my] secondary music teacher. I heard Kodály's *Hary Janos* and was amazed by the sound as well as the 'visuals' of a live orchestra. It was this (age about 12 I think) that I believe got me interested in taking music lessons—piano—and things took off from there.'

Performing in concerts, albeit maybe not on quite such a large scale, was also a prominent memory:

'I loved singing in the school choir and will always remember singing *Jonah Man Jazz* and other such musicals!'

' . . . learning the recorder and playing it in a festival with dozens of other children in Brian Bonsor's *Beguine*—it was thrilling to be in such a big group with what sounded such jazzy and catchy music.'

'Playing percussion and drums in county orchestras; my first big memory was playing the *James Bond Theme* and getting the drum fills right, which got me a fair bit of praise and pushed my playing onwards. Playing gigs generally at a young-ish age is such an eye-opener to another world.'

A pervasive theme throughout the questionnaire responses is the importance of music as a 'social' experience, seen here in:

'When I went to school (age 5, 1976) I loved singing in assembly, being part of something bigger than just me.'

'Some of my first times sleeping away from home were on musical adventures—orchestra weeks, school music trips/tours abroad, which cemented my view of music as a sociable activity.'

However, not all experiences were pleasurable—albeit still formative—and one person wrote about the necessity of 'Learning not to love music!' when taught the piano by a 'fierce' aunt and only being released from practice 'when the kitchen timer pinged!'

Another for whom piano lessons were obviously less than inspiring recounted an early incident thus:

'Writing a letter to Felix Swinstead (*Step by Step to the Classics*) at the age of 10 saying how miserable he was making my life and couldn't he produce a lesser form of torture. My mum just stopped me posting it . . . '

And one of the respondents suffered the unfortunately well-known experience of being 'told I couldn't sing when aged 7, heart broken.'

3. What do you think were the most important 'milestones' in your musical development, and why?

There was much response to this and some very extensive answers. It was possibly one of the questions that caused respondents to reflect most deeply, with one person commenting, 'Difficult question.' It was interpreted in different ways, with some people taking a narrative chronological approach:

'First LP. First live concert. First musical gig.'

'Passing all my violin exams 1–8 and music theory grade 5.'

The exam grade structure of assessment in fact cropped up in 13% of answers (reflecting the demographic of many of the respondents). They were perceived as ways of externally demonstrating progression and of helping build confidence—or the opposite: 'I did grade 1 piano but it was clearly so traumatic that I was never put in for another . . .'

Acquisition of particular 'technical' skills provided markers on the journey: playing by ear, reading chord symbols, improvising, writing songs, accessing technology to compose and record . . .

Some people traced a route through the phases of their musical life, picking out the highlights at each stage, as in the following example:

- Joining local church choir; I have loved vocal music especially since starting piano lessons; my active musical interests took off from that point really quite fast
- Watching the film *Fantasia* (seriously)—this really got me into listening to records and broadening repertoire

- Attendance at my first live 'gig'—Genesis in 1974—mind-blowing
- Going to college (St John's College, York) and mixing with other practising musicians
- Being a singer in St Edmundsbury Cathedral Choir—becoming a 'professional' in the 'quality' sense of my music-making

Others recounted specific experiences—critical incidents—that had changed their pathway, including changing schools and/or teachers:

'Moving to my second piano teacher who had more modern ideas on teaching—more flexibility, more drive, more possibilities.'

This potential for opening doors was mentioned by more than one person:

'Really liking a music teacher I had in Year 10 for a year and my A level music teacher. These were kind people and they were ambitious for me—they knew me and they wanted me to have good musical experiences . . . Because they knew me I didn't need to be pushy to be given things to do that I might like to do. I could be myself.'

Similarly, a new conservatoire teacher 'was refreshingly casual about exams/ college procedures and emphasized the importance of striving to be a great musical communicator, with my own voice and tried to teach me how to define and pursue what matters most to me as a musician. Studying with him has forever changed my outlook on what/why/how I do what I do as a musician.'

Other significant events included joining choirs, orchestras and other groups and, again, playing in concerts: 'I played a concerto at school which was scary but thrilling.'

Several experiences managed to be both positive and negative, not necessarily in that order, in ways that changed the course of the individual's journey:

'Going to junior conservatoire—immense opportunity to play/perform/ develop, while at same time completely putting you off wanting to study at music college full time!'

'At the age of 11 I failed the 11 Plus. This would turn out to be the most significant event on my whole musical development. As a result I went to the local Secondary Modern School where I came into contact with a marvellous young teacher . . . '

Do not imagine everyone's experiences of 'formal' music education in these answers were good ones. For one person, the only milestone given was 'training as a community musician at the age of 21—this helped me overcome the damage done by bad and boring music education'.

Rather than specific events, some people described broader periods, especially at secondary school and in higher education, that led to more generalized changes in, for example, their perception of music. For example, realizing 'the personal and social aspects of musical activity' and '. . . that music was both an expressive outlet and an intellectual challenge'. Respondents talked of increased confidence ('confidence in my own musicality'), of gaining independence, and of 'finding people who thought like me'.

One of the reasons the responses to this question were often so extensive (reflected in the length of this part of the report) is possibly because the journey is perceived by many people as continuous and ongoing:

> 'My music is still developing—my most recent milestone is at nearly 50 realizing I have the skills to develop other musicians and conduct choirs!'

> 'And I still eagerly await the next milestone, hooked on music as I am.'

4. Who have you learnt most from, and why?

Most people referred to teachers, in the sense of instrumental and school teachers or HE lecturers, as representing those from whom they had learned most, but there were also individuals beyond that, summarized in:

> 'I don't think I could narrow it down to one person; there have been so many incredibly inspiring people that I have worked with and learnt from . . . my parents . . . some incredible instrumental teachers . . . leading music workshop leaders . . . my peers.'

Of course, in a sense one could argue that anyone from whom one has 'learned' is therefore a 'teacher' and family featured strongly again, with one respondent writing 'My son, as he has a very eclectic taste in music and keeps me listening to things I probably wouldn't normally listen to. He stops me getting into a musical 'rut'.' While for one mostly self-taught respondent, the answer had to be 'self'.

Otherwise there were teachers at all phases of education and in various settings, including instrumental teachers, teachers in primary and secondary schools, higher education lecturers and PGCE mentors. A frequent explanation for the influence of these people was that they had been interested in their students for themselves:

> 'My piano teacher . . . a real concentration on musicianship and working with what skills I had as a musician rather than trying to make me into something that I wasn't.'

> ' . . . piano teacher . . . was interested in me as a whole musician, not which grade I was going to take next. Even though I was never going to be the best pianist in the world, she treated my learning as being of huge importance.'

> 'One very influential teacher was almost more of a life-coach.'

> 'It is . . . psychologically powerful to work on a regular basis with someone who has an unconditional positive regard for one's ability and character. This has been very good for my self-esteem.'

Several current teachers identified their own students (in whatever phase) as the biggest inspiration: 'Their creativity knows no bounds or preconceptions'.

Colleagues and peers were also recognized:

> 'The no.1 at my first job . . . I have used the skills I learned there continuously ever since . . . The head teacher [there], who understood that the school's elite atmosphere was not for me and encouraged me to move into primary school music.'

> 'My librettists who have stretched me'.

> 'My singing friends. That creating music together can be a most wonderful and joyful shared experience'.

> 'My peers. They allowed me to make my own musical decisions and be creative'.

> 'In one amateur orchestra in which I played over several years I shared the front desk with the section's paid professional leader . . . I learned a tremendous amount from him: for me every orchestra rehearsal was a cello lesson.'

> 'Other musicians on the Teaching Music website [www.teaching.music. org.uk] for ideas and responses to forums.'

Many people named notable figures who had influenced them at different stages of their musical journey. There were musicians past: 'I've learned most from J.S. Bach. No other music touches my soul & spirit like his' and present: Andre Previn (via TV), the violinist Frederick Grinke, and saxophonists Warne Marsh and Jerry Kellock. From the music education world, the most frequently cited influence was Keith Swanwick 'his work underpins everything I know about what is important in music education', but John Paynter, Arnold Bentley, Jan Holdstock (whose own pathway is included elsewhere in this book) George Odam and Janet Mills, among others, also make appearances.

The title to this chapter comes from one answer that included several of the above aspects: 'I have learned a lot by spending quality time with instruments. My singing teacher . . . has been a huge influence and mostly my musical peers. I am learning all the time.'

5. What do you consider to be your most important musical skills, and how did you learn them?

Although the answers here were shorter than in previous sections, nevertheless most people picked several key skills, even though there were accompanying comments such as 'Actually it's very hard to isolate musical skills like this!' There was some overlap, especially with question 8, as respondents often chose what was useful to them in a teaching situation—not surprising given the importance of music in many of these people's careers.

The aspect identified most frequently in this section was that of sightreading/sightsinging—chosen by about 22%.

> 'Sight reading has been a boon. I learnt this through not practising as much as I could and trying to blag my way through piano lessons.'

> '. . . general practice has enabled me to develop these skills over time.'

> 'I have always excelled at this due to the constant studying of new music from a young age'

> 'Always been quite good, but choral singing has really helped with that and orchestral scratch days'

Listening was identified as important by nearly 18% and was frequently spoken of in association with linked aspects, for instance evaluating, responding, being an integral part of making music with others and concentration:

> 'I should say that being able to listen and accompany has been one of my most important skills. To be able to slot into a situation, with any different combination of musicians and be able to keep it together professionally. I think it's developed through lots of exposure to playing in ensembles from an early age.'

> 'Being able to listen and critically evaluate musical outcomes'

> 'I think my most important musical skill is being able to respond musically to what others are doing around me. This involves a lot of listening, and being open to anything.'

> 'Concentration. Is that a musical skill? I hope so. Perhaps I mean listening.'

A knowledge of the repertoire, composing and conducting skills were important for some people, while technical instrumental and vocal skills were also valued, alongside associated skills such as, in the case of instruments, improvising and accompanying; and in the case of vocal activities, harmonization. These 'secondary' skills had often been learnt in practice or on the job rather than having been taught specifically or discretely.

As seen above, personal skills, such as concentration, also featured. Among other aspects in this category were

> 'Patience and humour, which are life skills really.'

> 'The ability to explain potentially complicated concepts in an accessible way . . .'

'communication',

'openmindedness'

'observation skills'

'Enthusiasm and spontaneity'

6. What factors have influenced your choice of music-making activities?

Most of the respondents were motivated to make music through a sense of personal enjoyment, satisfaction and well-being, and this drove them on, even when circumstances were not favourable. While some referred to inhibiting factors such as pressure of work or families, others were clearly determined to take whatever opportunities presented themselves: 'I live in an isolated rural community and there's no such thing as an orchestra . . . but there is a good choir, and joining this [a] few years ago has been a tremendous addition to my life.'

Again, playing with others is important for many people—'an inherent need to make music with others' as one person described it—to the extent that the choice of activities sometimes depended on being available at a particular time, 'I started playing in the jazz band because I met someone when their last bass player had just left'. However, the importance of feeling comfortable within a music-making group could also influence people's choices negatively, as with the following player: 'I have joined orchestras in the past and left after a few rehearsals because people have been so unwilling to welcome new people.'

For some, as seen in answers to the first question, tastes and preferences were shaped early in their lives:

'I started on the piano because we had one and my dad played.'

'. . . seeing a brass band as a child and wanting to be able to play the music they were playing'

These early experiences could sometimes be limiting:

'I regret that at the time I received my formal music education, neither improvisation nor playing by ear was an essential part of the curriculum. I have little confidence doing either.'

Teachers sometimes found their activities were influenced by the needs of their work:

'. . . recently, the interests and abilities of the children with whom I work have been the deciding factor.'

7. When and why did you decide to become involved in music education?

[Not relevant to all respondents]

Just over 70 of the 85 responses were from people involved in music education. Of these, a significant number (17%) said music teaching was something they had always wanted to do, or had decided on at an early age. One of these individuals came from a teaching family: 'I used to observe my dad teach when I had inset days from school and became very excited by this process.'

For others, the impetus came from their own experiences of music education, whether positive:

> 'I wanted to influence in the same way that [my teacher] had and encourage young people to gain a love of music and music-making.'

or negative:

> 'I reflected on how bad secondary class music lessons had been. I wanted a better deal for children.'

For about 25%, the decision to go into music teaching was made around the time of their university course:

> 'I loved music and studied a music degree. I did quite a lot of peripatetic teaching whilst a student and so a PGCE with a specialism in music followed.'

> 'I always knew that I wanted to be a teacher, but it was not until University that I realized that I wanted to teach music.'

Some didn't make a deliberate career choice, but still got hooked!

> 'Couldn't think of anything else to do at first. Then got my first job and really enjoyed it.'

Others came into teaching from other careers or after having had children of their own:

> 'I had a 'day job' which was leaving me feeling unfulfilled, so I took the plunge and trained in secondary education.'

The desire to 'pass on my enthusiasm about music to others' features strongly, as does the idea of working creatively with young people:

> 'sharing my passion for music and giving pupils the opportunity to be creative in the classroom'

> 'I loved working with children and I loved the creative process.'

8. What do you consider to be your most effective teaching skills and how did you develop them?

[Not relevant to all respondents]

This question, perhaps predictably, gave rise to a wide range of responses from those involved in music education, the sum total of which could easily be turned into a manual of good teaching practice! A lot of responses focused on an ability to build good relationships and develop a rapport with students. There was a recognition of the importance of a 'desire to relate to young people and communicate with them', of 'seeing things from the students' point of view' and of having 'empathy with learners'. One said: 'I simply love and enjoy being surrounded by children'.

Many cited building self-esteem, 'giving people belief in their ability to do more than they ever thought possible' and 'instilling a belief that they can do it'. The importance of giving appropriate praise and encouragement was frequently mentioned. This is an interesting reflection of the number of times confidence was mentioned in answers to earlier questions.

Some referred to the ability to 'facilitate & encourage learning' and 'knowing when to step back and let people do things for themselves'. One teacher referred to 'joy in helping people to do things and to discover things in their own way' and another to 'trusting in human musicality'.

The ability to 'encourage . . . composition skills and creative music-making'—again, linking with findings from earlier questions—was seen as important. While several people, perhaps following Keith Swanwick's lead, stressed the importance of 'making a lesson a musical experience' or 'provid[ing] real musical experiences in the classroom'.

Several people mentioned the ability to 'make it fun' and to 'get students to enjoy and achieve', and effective motivational, communication and demonstration skills were often cited as being important. Others mentioned subject knowledge, creating good resources, planning and behaviour management.

The most frequently mentioned personal qualities were passion, enthusiasm, patience and fairness. Others mentioned openness to new ideas and allowing teaching and learning to go in unexpected directions. One teacher recognized the importance of 'staying true to myself, whatever context I am working in'.

Skills were mostly learnt through experience on the job, and respondents included acknowledgement of the support they received from other teachers. Trial and error and learning from mistakes were mentioned several times, while one person said, 'The students are my best teachers', again, echoing earlier answers.

9. How would you like your 'pathway' to continue? Where do you see yourself, musically, in five years' time?

The overwhelming impression is that people want to do more music, to improve their playing and (for those in education) develop their understanding of teaching and learning. Some mentioned specific goals such as learning to play a new instrument, joining an orchestra, band or choir, doing more of their own composition or gaining qualifications. Some, in the early stages of their careers, had clear ideas of where they wanted to go in the future. Others expressed regret that their work (whether in music education or elsewhere) was preventing them from making as much music as they would like to.

Responses included:

> 'I hope that I'll still be making music and that I'll continue to grasp any music-making opportunities that come my way.'

> 'I would like to do far more playing.'

> 'Spending more time making music myself.'

> 'I would like to develop the 'playing from ear skill'.'

> 'Hopefully still singing. I'd love to be singing to my grandchildren long into my old age!'

> 'I would like to learn more about music technology.'

> 'I would like to be more involved in developing pedagogy and practice for music teachers.'

> 'I do want to be inspiring and enthusing children about how much fun and personal enjoyment (not to mention a sense of achievement) they can get through music.'

> 'Hopefully I will be a better teacher, exploring new ways to communicate music and enabling young people to have a fulfilling experience of music.'

The overall impression is of people who are very committed to their music-making and, for those in education, to their role in providing musical opportunities for others. '[I]n five years I hope we could look back and say, "Yes we made a difference".'

10. Is there anything else you would like to add in relation to your own experience?

This resulted in a wide range of answers, some highlighting issues that the respondents thought were particularly important, others summarizing their attitudes to music and music-making.

Some people were concerned about the place of music in the curriculum:

> 'It is vital that music remain a core part of the curriculum and school life.'

> '. . . it is a right for everyone to enjoy.'

Others recognized the importance of their early musical experiences in their own lives:

'I am the first musician in my family and had I not had access to musical learning at primary school . . . I would not have the job I have today.'

Once again, a number emphasized the importance of making music with others:

'I don't think I can stress enough the importance of group music-making.'

'Singing with others makes one feel good.'

'I am still inspired by musicians that I meet, so feel in a way I am still "growing" musically.'

Many used this question to emphasize the important place of music in their lives. One referred to the 'healing power of music' and another said '[music] changed my life for ever'. An eloquent description of the value of music comes in this response:

'There was a long time in my life when I did no music at all. Looking back they were some of the unhappiest years of my life. Singing . . . always lifts my spirits and has allowed me to meet and engage with some remarkable people. I know that I cannot exist without music.'

This final response returns us to the book's theme:

'It's been a great journey and I can't wait to see what happens next!'

Summary

The breadth and variety of response is clearly demonstrated above, even in this necessarily compact account. The ability of music to underpin and permeate people's personal and professional lives is apparent; as is the commitment and care of those involved in education. There is much we can learn and reaffirm from considering how the routes of those further along their musical journeys can inform the provision we help construct for those at an earlier stage.

In this survey we can see several overarching factors — some long-term, some one-off — that seem to have had particularly formative effects on the musical pathways of those involved. Although there may be nothing particularly new in the following, nevertheless it is salutary to have them confirmed in such a powerful way:

- The influence of family in providing and 'normalizing' a context that supports musical experience and development
- The potential of schools to provide a range of personal and musical opportunities, including extra-curricular
- Teachers and mentors at all phases and in all areas of musical experience who are concerned for the all-round development of the pupil as an individual, building confidence and self-esteem

- The existence of a network such as local area music schools that can provide more extensive opportunities for teaching/learning and participation
- Peers and colleagues who share the same interests
- Being taken to large scale concerts at an early age
- Performing in concerts, festivals and competitions—especially in groups larger than normally experienced

And, finally:

- Music itself, with its power to move and enthral; perceived and encountered as a social activity, drawing together people in a unique shared experience.

Acknowledgements

With many thanks to all those who contributed to the questionnaire—your thoughtful responses were more (in all senses!) than we could have hoped for.

'Sinning in the barth': primary children as musicians

Lis McCullough

'When I was 3 I was sinning in the barth and I was sinning dinamit'
(Owen, Year 3)

When some of the pupils in a primary school were asked whether they would like to contribute to a book about musical pathways, it is not surprising that they were keen to be involved. The children in a Year 3 (ages 7–8) and a Year 5 (ages 9–10) class took part during two of their normal weekly music sessions. There is a lot of music in this school. As well as the normal class music times, all children learn recorders in Year 2 as part of the Wider Opportunities scheme and many learn instruments both in and out of school (violin, cello, guitar, flute, oboe, clarinet, percussion, piano . . .) during Key Stage 2. There is regular singing in assemblies; the orchestra, wind band and other instrumental groups play frequently to the rest of the school and to parents; and there are major musical 'events' at celebrations such as Harvest Festival and Christmas.

A duplicated sheet consisting of various 'pointers', based on the original adult questionnaire on the NAME website, was used with both classes, separately, as the framework for an initial group discussion about the theme of musical pathways. It covered first musical memories; the sorts of musical involvement the children had had to date in and out of school; particular skills they had gained; people who had helped them; and what they thought their musical involvement might be in the future—at secondary school, as an adult, and in their careers. Although this sheet was then used as a check sheet by the Year 5s when writing their individual responses, most of the Year 3s found it easier to write about/draw themselves as musicians in the past, the present and the future.

The next sections summarize some of the main points arising from the children's accounts, illustrated by short quotes, with some of the contributions then being given in full. It should be remembered that, although there was initial discussion, what the children wrote was not verbally followed up. It should also be remembered that, especially for the Year 3s, writing down what they thought was harder than speaking about it, so what they wrote is likely to reflect what they *could* write, rather than being necessarily a full depiction of their thoughts. Spelling and some punctuation have been 'standardized', except for Owen whose sentence about singing *Dynamite* in the bath was too good to miss for a title!

First memories

> 'My first musical memory is when I was little and in front of the TV when the Teletubbies theme tune came on'

(Darby, Year 5)

The children spoke readily of their musical involvement. They were particularly taken with the concept of having a 'first musical memory' and there was much discussion and most response about this. We talked about what the word 'musical' might mean, in the sense of what sorts of activities it might encompass and the first memories expressed by these children were overwhelmingly to do with **playing instruments**:

My first musical memory . . .

> '. . . was when I was 3 and I liked playing random notes on the guitar. And my dad plays it too' (Lewis, Year 3)

> '. . . was when my dad went to London and got me a [pan]pipe instrument' (Jasmine, Year 3)

> '. . . was when I started playing the keyboard when I was 3' (Georgia, Year 5)

> '. . . when I got a pink and white polka dot mini guitar for Christmas 5 years ago. I like music because it's very flowy and it's like swimming' (Maisie A, Year 5)

> 'When I was four I got my first guitar and recorded myself. And I was at the seaside' (Harry, Year 3)

> 'My first music experience was when I got my first maracas and I used to play them every day and make new tunes' (Holly, Year 5)

> 'I first played the drums when I was 4. I played a loud tune and that's when I got into it' (Lewis A, Year 5)

> 'When I was five I got my first guitar for Christmas. I strummed it all day long' (Robert, Year 5)

Several of the children talked of being attracted to a particular instrument because of the sound it made:

> 'I enjoy the sound of the guitar (Robert, Year 5)

> 'I do enjoy playing the guitar . . . I enjoy the sound of the guitar' (Harry, Year 5)

> 'I don't play an instrument but I think I would like the flute because it makes a nice sound' (Molly, Year 5)

This attraction to the sound of an instrument, together with exploring the instrument, reflect the findings that contributed to the first level of the Swanwick Tillman developmental spiral (Swanwick & Tillman, 1986).

However, as with Owen's opening quote above, there were also some early memories related to **singing**, either their own or others':

'My first musical memory was when my brothers were singing' (Molly, Year 5)

'When I was a baby my dad said he put a song on and I started singing' (Finlay, Year 5)

'My first music memory is pop. When I first heard it I liked it' (Aiden, Year 5)

Picture 1: Evie's first musical memory

There were also several memories relating to **dance**:

> 'My first musical memory is when I used to breakdance in front of the tv' (Regan, Year 5)

> '. . . was when I was about 3/4 I did a little Irish jig and I fell over while I was doing it but I still enjoyed it and had lots of fun and I have carried on ever since' (Cait, Year 3)

> '. . . Dancing in my bedroom with the radio on' (Thomas A, Year 3)

> 'When I was little I—well it's a bit embarrassing—I used to dance to *Can't get you out of my head* by Kylie Minogue. I shaked my legs, head and arms and my family used to go round and round the table with me on their shoulders' (Maisie B, Year 5)

Influences

As can be seen from the above, many early influences came, not surprisingly, from close family. Some children were specific:

> 'I was interested in music when I saw my dad played the guitar' (Robert, Year 5)

> 'When my brother showed me a band called Tenacious D' (Darby, Year 5)

> 'My first musical memory was when my sister played her flute' (Lewis B, Year 5)

> My first musical experience was when I went to my auntie's house and got an accordion off the shelf and started playing . . . I heard my uncle play and that inspired me to involve music in my life . . . I sang in a talent contest and my auntie introduced me to Vampire Weekend (a US indie band). My auntie and uncle have been a massive part of my life when it comes to music from introducing me to bands to helping me play music. (William, Year 5)

> My first memory is when my mum lifted me on the piano stool and I would start to play. Well, my mum is a musician so she inspired me to play piano. My mum is still a music teacher so that kept me going . . . I like Mozart and Bach but I don't want to be a musician [when I grow up] but I will keep playing. (Andrew, Year 5)

Current teachers were also mentioned, for example Harry (Year 5) considered his guitar teacher had been a particularly supportive influence 'because he's fun and he understands me.' The implicit role of the school in presenting opportunities and options—particularly in relation to instruments—cropped up frequently.

Present musical involvement

'In year 5 I started to play the drums and now I am playing the drums and the guitar.' (Issy, Year 5)

The emphasis on instruments as the dominant aspect of musical involvement continued for those who included aspects about themselves in the present and the future. For example, Thomas B's first musical memory followed through into his current involvement:

'My musical memory was when I first learnt flute at school. I enjoyed it so much. I still learn flute today and I am very good at it. These are the notes B, A, G, C, B♭, E, F, F♯, low D, high D.' (Year 3)

And he illustrated this with 'before' and 'after' pictures of himself with curved and standard head joints, together with staff notation for the itemized notes.

'A week ago I got a keyboard with a book for 50p. And my brother can play *Jingle bells*. And I have a guitar and I have drums' (Billy, Year 3).

Picture 2: 'Playing my electric guitar at home. I started playing when I was 6 at guitar lessons. My first song was *Twinkle little star*' (Thomas A, Year 3).

For many children, the word 'memory' from the first question then became a term marking the next stages (present and future), even when what was being described was not (yet) a memory as such, see, for example, the account by Neve (Year 3) below.

Picture 3: Neve's past, present and future as a musician

Interestingly, although Neve (Year 3) sees singing as part of being a musician, this was not always the case (mirroring some findings in Alexandra Lamont's chapter in this book). For example, Aaron (Year 5) wrote, 'I love singing . . . Music's OK but singing is much better.'

For Emma (Year 5), see below, catchy words—as well as the singers—make music interesting, so pop music is rated more highly than 'really boring' classical music.

Perhaps that helps explain why, for those who expressed preference in music, it was often popular singers who were identified. For example, Aaron (Year 5) wrote that 'My favourite singers are JLS, Tinie Tempah and Bruno Mars' while Finlay (Year 5) named 'Eminem, Wiz Khalifa, Mann, Chris Brown'.

Anticipating the future

'In the future I am going to sing on my own.' (Kacey, Year 3)

For some children there was a continuation from present activities, for example, Joshua A (Year 3) wrote 'First memory. My first instrument was playing the piano. The future. Me playing in an orchestra.' And drew pictures to accompany this.

For others the future was seen as an opportunity to do something different:

'When I get older I [am] going to play an electric guitar' (Joshua B, Year 3).

Some children anticipated they might have a career in music — especially the pop world:

'When I am older I will be a rock star' (Luca, Year 3)

While James (Year 5) outlined his anticipated musical journey as follows

Future: Singer — Famous
Past: Drummer
Present: Singer — Drummer
Secondary school: DJ, Singer
College: DJ — Singer
University: Singer

Although others saw it more as a leisure activity, for example Andrew (Year 5) above, who wrote about not wanting to be a musician, although he would keep playing.

Musical pathways

There follow some of the more extended pieces, many of which demonstrate similar aspects to those mentioned above.

> When I was 3 I got a keyboard. I learnt to play it in a few months. I started recorder at 6. I learnt to play it and at 8 I got a guitar. Now I still learn it. Singing is fun and I like listening to it. The flute is another instrument I learnt to play. When I'm older I would like to play guitar in a band. (Katy, Year 3)

Now:
'I have an instrument and it is a flute. I know some notes called A, B, G, C, F, E and D. At home I sing with my brother. I sometimes get my brother's guitar and play on it.'

Past:
My [first] musical memory is when I saw my mum in a band. (Tilley, Year 3)

My first musical memory was when I was five and I started singing. When I was seven I started playing piano and I was really excited. I also started playing the trumpet when I was seven. I am still doing all of those things. When I am older I am going to start my own band! (Amber-Jade, Year 3)

My first musical memory was when I was walking into assembly when I was in Year 1 and the orchestra was playing and I really liked the sound.

What interested me in doing the drums was when I heard them play in the drum assembly. I also play the violin and I was interested in that by the sound of it in the orchestra and the violin assembly.

When I was in Year 2 the whole class learnt the recorder. When it finished I carried on playing. I have now gone on to playing the tenor recorder.

My favourite type of music is pop music because I like the artists who sing them. But I don't like classical music because there are no words and it's really boring. I really like pop music because it has lots of words to learn and they are very catchy.

My mum is always encouraging me to try hard in music and do my best.

In Year 2 I had no music sense at all, but now I am in Year 5 and my third year of music I have picked up a lot more information than I did.

I am always going to do my music and I hope I never give up. (Emma, Year 5)

My first musical memory is when I was about 3 years old and I was at my nan's house and she taught me how to play *Twinkle twinkle little star* on the piano. From then on I have always played the piano. Now when I sleep at my nan's she is teaching me to play *Für Elise*. Last year (2010) I joined a piano class. Since I was 2 I have loved to dance. I go to Mayhem Theatre Arts and I love to do tap, street, modern and lots more. I often do shows. When my school did Roselands Got Talent I entered as a solos act and I didn't win, but I tried my hardest and I still got a medal for unique talent. I listen to lots of different types of music like hip hop etc. (Maddison, Year 5)

When I was 4 I performed at my mum's wedding. This year, 2011, I performed in Roselands Got Talent. I sang *The Lazy Song*. I love singing — I've loved it since I was 4. At the moment my favourite song is *Spaceship* by Dappy and Tinchy Stryder. One day I hope to be in a band. The biggest audience I've ever played in front of is in the Roselands Got Talent final. If I get to a band when I'm older I will always remember the Roselands Got Talent final. (Oliver, Year 5)

My first musical memory was my brother used to sing to me when I was younger.

I started playing the flute in Year 4 because I tried it and I loved playing it. But I'm not carrying on. My flute is a nice tune and I love playing it … and it brings joy to me. I've learnt loads of songs. My favourite one [is] *Awake my love*. I've just learnt it.

In Year 2 I learnt the recorder and I loved it. It is good joy and you learn loads of notes and you have to remember all the notes you've learnt.

My favourite songwriter is Bruno Mars because he writes lots of songs I love. I sometimes just come out with songs that are in my head.

In the future I want to do something with music. I want to still play the flute but I can't. I want to be a beautician and a hairdresser and I want to play the violin. (Anna, Year 5)

My first music memory was when I got a drum kit for Christmas when I was a toddler.

What made me interested in music was when we had a music assembly when I was in Year 2. I thought the clarinet was interesting so I picked it.

When I completed my Grade 1 that kept me going because I passed.

When I took part in the music at the Christmas concert that was a special event.

[My clarinet teacher], my mum and dad have supported me and encouraged me to play the clarinet.

What I've done: I know how to make high sounds come out of my clarinet.

My favourite music: I like clarinet music and R and B music. I also like pop music too.

My career: I wouldn't really pick music as my career when I'm older, but I'll still make a few pieces of music for my clarinet now and then. (Chloe, Year 5)

My first musical memory was at Christmas in 2008 when I had asked for a violin and my nan got me one. I was soooo happy.

My favourite music is pop and I'm not really into classical or opera because they're slow and boring. And you can't really dance to it.

I was interested in music especially the violin because my auntie is very musical and has been in many orchestras and has played the violin on so many stages even in Scotland.

I have done my prep test and I have done my Grade 1 and I got a merit and now I am working on my Grade 2 for violin and so far it's pretty easy.

When I joined my school orchestra it helped me and that has helped me get a merit in violin Grade 1 . . . I do violin on a Monday 3 times in 1 day. (Trinity, Year 5)

My first musical memory was when my sister wasn't playing on her keyboard I would press the keys and just have fun. My second memory was when I did my audition on Roselands Got Talent. Because I played my cello at the beginning [and] I got a special award [Ed.: for the originality of her act, which combined cello playing and gymnastics!]

Interest in making music: I think music is an enjoyable hobby and some sort of career might be ahead.

My musical skills: I play the cello and I'm taught by the amazing Mr T. S. He's really made me enjoy music. My music teacher Mrs M. I am taught by at school. She is very helpful in my musical sense.

I learnt the cello because I had no idea what it was.' (Amber, Year 5)

---

1. My first musical memory was when I was little and I saw a band play and I really liked the sound of the instruments.

2. The thing that made me interested in music was when I heard the flutes play Wallace and Gromit.

3. I perform in orchestra and I'm in a flute choir, which means I play in assemblies and when it's the flute assembly.

4. I listen to R & B music. I love to sing and play the flute.

5. When I grow up I want to be a singer or an actor.

Rebecca (Year 5)

Final thoughts

Although it has not been possible to include all the responses, from the examples above it is obvious that these children were able to engage with the idea of having an ongoing musical life and express aspects that they considered part of it. They understood that not only could they get better at what they did, but that there were also opportunities for other areas of musical involvement. Whatever their earliest memories from the past, their participation and preferences in the present and their anticipated musical involvement in the future, what we hope for them and for everyone else is that they should be able to say, 'I feel happy with my musical life.' (Joey, Year 5)

Acknowledgements

With many thanks to the head teacher, staff and pupils at Roselands Primary School and apologies to all those whose words and pictures could not be included.

References

Swanwick, K. and Tillman J. (1986) The sequence of musical development: A study of children's composition. *British Journal of Music Education* 3(3): 305–339.

Section 3

Individual Pathways

Between today and yesterday (is like a million years . . .)

David Ashworth

I remember first becoming interested, very interested, in music when I was about 11 or 12. The music coming out of the radio started to grab my attention. I didn't know what it was—I just liked the sound it made. There was—there is—something magical about putting together drums, bass guitar and electric guitars. Add voices with American or Liverpool accents and it gets even better. There was also the compelling sound of acoustic guitars—strummed or finger style, doesn't matter—it sounds great both ways. Add a harmonica and a nasal voice with some far out lyrics . . . wow, what is going on here? How do I get under the bonnet?

I was lucky. I lived in a small, isolated market town in Cumbria, but there were others, similarly stricken by these sounds, living on the same street. Down the road, a lad a year or two older than me had put down his acoustic guitar in favour of an electric guitar and he was kind enough to lend me the discarded instrument—my times they were a-changing while his homesick blues went subterranean. A friend further up the road was having guitar lessons, learning to be the next Hank Marvin. He taught me the chords in return for me accompanying his lead playing. Flingel Bunt rose and fell. Soon we were hungry for more. There was just the one record shop in town and it had a leaning towards the classical. The owner did stock some pop music, but only ordered one copy of each album. So there was just one copy of *Highway 61 Revisited*, just the one *Sgt Pepper* up for grabs. We managed to track down the lucky owners of these seminal albums. Word soon spread around and you would see a steady pilgrimage of young people (armed with tape recorders) beating a path to the houses of the chosen few. So music in those early years was very much a communal experience—making and sharing music with friends.

Then there was 'school music'. This was something very different and I made no connection between it and my music-making outside. I remember nothing of classroom music lessons, but I did enjoy playing violin (badly) in the school orchestra. I just loved the idea of so many people making music together—I still do.

But there was one key milestone during those school years. The music teacher was very much 'old school' but he kept his eyes and ears open. He realized that there were increasing numbers of students desperate to learn the guitar—an instrument that neither he nor the music service knew anything about. So he drafted me in to teach younger students how to play—during lunchtimes and after school. He even let us perform in some school concerts. This was huge fun. But in a sense it was too late. I was doing maths, further maths and physics and sliding down the slippery scientific slope . . .

Then came university. Wow! OK, I had the misfortune to be doing a science degree, but the musical opportunities were endless—early-music sessions, folk clubs and countless informal jam sessions, working with jazz musicians, Indian musicians, electronics and tape loops, and poetry and folk evenings. There were parties in student flats with the music of Frank Zappa, Neil Young, John Fahey, Family, The Doors . . . heady stuff. My musical horizons were starting to explode . . .

Fast-forward a few years. I'm teaching maths in a secondary school in York, but they've let me have the Sixth Form General Studies music slot. This was working with students who were interested in music but not following the classically-based curriculum on offer. This was a problem in the 1970s. I did the only thing possible. I bought a book. I struck lucky—very lucky. Vulliamy and Lee's *Pop Music in School* (1976) was way ahead of its time. Chapter headings included 'the creative possibilities of pop', 'pupil-centred music teaching' and 'running an "open" music department'. Time for a major career change, methinks. After intensive late night and weekend study, courses, Open University summer schools and an ABRSM Diploma, I was ready to go.

The only problem was the large gulf between the music teaching I had to offer and what schools and the music service were prepared to accept. They were still subscribing heavily to the western classical tradition—ain't no room in there for a guitar man. So I started doing some teaching on the fringes and went back to my Vulliamy and Lee book. The writers and series editors were based at York University—up the road. I rang the University switchboard and asked to speak to someone from the music department. Two hours later, I was sitting in John Paynter's office. Three hours later, life had changed for the better. John outlined his vision for practical, classroom-based music-making that placed creativity at the centre—and the important steps he was taking to make this happen.

Inspired by this, I began my 'portfolio' career in music education. This involved a wide range of activities including:

- Directing and performing in various ensembles
- Co-founding a publishing company for which I wrote and published educational materials
- Establishing a teaching studio and leading a team providing tuition and workshop support to schools and the informal sector
- Leading summer schools and workshops exploring songwriting, improvisation and group composition

These pathways eventually converged when I took up a post with City of York Council as their music consultant. Throughout this time, I was taking forward and implementing two of John Paynter's key principles: music is about getting excited by sounds; and music can only be said to be truly happening when people are making it.

I have always tried to find sounds that will inspire young people to want to make music. After all, that is what got me hooked in the first place. This can be difficult in schools. High-quality instruments, and players who can bring the best sounds out of them, are often in short supply. I therefore started to explore the various ways in which technology can be used to provide an extended palette of sounds. And because

I prefer to put the emphasis on live music-making (as opposed to recording), I tended to favour the use of samplers and sound processors over computers.

The opportunity to extend this work came when I took up a three-year post as NAME's Lead Consultant for ICT—leading a Becta-funded contract on embedding ICT in the music curriculum. I was able to explore the interesting work that was and is going on all over the country and share these ideas nationally. A key milestone during this time came with the opportunity to publish *Electrifying Music: a guide to using ICT in music education* in 2007.

Working with Musical Futures provided me with the opportunity to explore online social networking and help with the development of NUMU. I also became project leader for the Teaching Music website (www.teachingmusic.org.uk). As more of my work began to centre on helping teachers and students share and collaborate online, I was able to return full circle and move back to Cumbria. From my base in the hills, I am still able to play a full and active part in music education locally and nationally. I am fortunate enough to be able to combine work in local schools with consultancy work for national organizations.

It has been a long and winding road, but we are now in a world where the sort of music I want to teach and, more importantly, the way I want to teach it, are valued. We need to remember that what draws us to music in the first place is the sound it makes. It is the timbres and textures that draw me back again and again to such music as *Desolation Row*, Bartók's string quartets and *Waterloo Sunset*. If we can get our students hooked on sound, they will want to explore further and understand how music is put together. And they will want to go on learning well beyond their years at school. Our work in the classrooms should be about nurturing the beginning of longer musical journeys.

Thanks to all those key people who helped me on my musical journey, I'm now enjoying giving something back in a musical environment where there is much more diversity, openness and honesty in how we help young people on their chosen musical paths.

References

Ashworth, D. (2007) *Electrifying Music: A Guide to using ICT in Music Education.* London: Musical Futures.

Vulliamy, G. & Lee, E. (1976) *Pop Music in School.* Cambridge: Cambridge University Press.

From bike to BAFTA —
a musical journey

Linda Bance

1963. 'Mum can I play the violin?' I asked my mother one evening after school. Mr Waller, our headmaster, had been approached by the Great Yarmouth Music Service to give a music aptitude test to his pupils.

I passed the test and was told that I had 'perfect pitch' and was offered the opportunity to play the violin. My father was very concerned about this. He remembers cringing at the thought and told me that if I made the horrid noise that most violin pupils made when practising then I would have to give up. Maybe that was why I became so determined. Despite this, my family played a great part in encouraging me to persevere. Music was always being played in the house either on the BBC light programme or when my mum, dad and grandads played piano and harmonicas. We spent wonderful and memorable evenings playing together.

At school I really enjoyed the experience of playing alongside 10 others in the group lessons. After one term I was invited to have private lessons with Mr Croker, who was one of the local peripatetic teachers and a member of the Hallé Orchestra.

I soon joined Great Yarmouth Youth Orchestra and continued my musical career against all odds. I cycled and bussed everywhere for lessons and was the youngest and smallest member of the orchestra to visit Rambouillet in France. I was also a member of many music clubs which played for the community of Great Yarmouth. Sadly for me, I was the only violinist in my secondary modern school. This was not helpful for my 'street cred' as I cycled with my violin poking out of the back of my Moulton bike. I did not look cool, but I did not care.

When I was 13, my family moved to Oxfordshire where I was again the only violinist in school. Fitzharrys School in Abingdon was quite supportive of my passion but could not offer anything traditional in the way of orchestras, so I made it my job to learn other instruments that were more acceptable in the school. As a guitarist and recorder player I led a folk band called the Missfitz and enjoyed the performance aspect of playing for school concerts.

In order for me to continue playing the violin I began private lessons, at great expense for my parents, at the Abingdon School of Music. I played first violin for the North Berkshire Youth Orchestra, led at the time by Anthony Le Fleming. Anthony was very helpful in getting me lessons and we travelled far and wide with the orchestra. I loved it and spent every waking hour playing music. Playing was my social life.

However, when it came to deciding my career path in the fifth form, to the dismay of both my parents and my head of year, I chose to become a nursery nurse over studying at the Royal College of Music. At the time, Berkshire was running a three-year course for nursery nursing, with a salary which enabled me to continue my violin playing as a hobby—and I reached Grade 7.

It was while I was at Saxon Road Nursery in Abingdon that I began to lead singing using my guitar. I listened carefully to the wise words of my head teacher, Miss Bristow, who told me to 'slow down and listen to the children', and I built a reputation of being the 'music person', which was unusual in a nursery. On a visit to Radio Oxford with my folk group, I met Margaret Shepherd. At the time, Margaret, along with Avril Holmes, was developing a pre-school music programme, *Sing a Song of Sixpence*, for Radio Oxford. Margaret invited me to sing with them and often visited the nursery where I was still a student, to record the children for the programme. This was the highlight of my work.

After completing my nursery nurse course I left the UK to work as a nanny in Geneva. For nearly five years I worked hard, rarely having time for much violin playing, but still using my music with young children and building a repertoire of folk songs and children's songs that always came in handy.

On my return to the UK, with my experience of music and languages, I began working in the nurseries of the European School in Culham, Oxfordshire. My musical skills were valuable there when using singing to help teach English as a foreign language. It was at this time that I met Lin Marsh, a musician and composer who encouraged me to develop my interests.

Imagine my excitement when, after the birth of my first child, Margaret Shepherd invited me to join a team of new parents and doctors whilst they carried out research for a documentary entitled *In Tune with Each Other.* The documentary highlighted the positive effect of singing on bonding with your new-born and the well-being of new parents and their young.

With our youngest daughter, I began to hold a few small music sessions, firstly in Margaret's sitting room and then in mine. When the classes grew, I was offered a place at Abingdon Music School running three music classes every Thursday morning. The classes were very popular, as it was very rare then to find such an activity. Margaret continued to support our work and promoted outreach into hospitals and clinics.

A few years later, my husband and I moved to Hertfordshire where I continued to run music classes for families with babies and children in their early years. When Margaret decided to retire she gave me the title of *Music with Mum*—the name with which she had been associated during her researching and working years. Suddenly I was extremely busy playing and running sessions every day of the week. I began to realize that I needed to know more. What was going on here? Why was it so popular? Who else was doing this? Clearly it was a very new idea to our region.

I became a member of the Pre-School Music Association (PRESMA), which is based in Norfolk, and this became a good source of sharing and a platform for discussion. At this point, I also joined Trinity College of Music to pursue the Certificate and Diploma in Music Education, focusing solely on music in the early years. This was a big challenge for me, as I was required to retake violin and theory exams. Early years was an unusual area for the conservatoire as, at the time, little had been researched or written on the subject. By the time I completed my Masters in Music Education, it was becoming a much more popular area of development.

After my graduation I became almost fully employed training, consulting or teaching music in the early years.

2011. I continue to work passionately in this area as a member of NAME and of MERYC (the European Network of Music Educators and Researchers of Young Children), and as music education consultant for the BAFTA-award-winning CBeebies programme ZingZillas.

Margaret Shepherd passed away recently, in her 94th year, and I owe much to her support and encouragement. I would say my pathway into music education was quite unusual and I am so proud to say that I began my career as a nursery nurse. With so many wonderful experts in this field now, I am still learning alongside them as we work to develop good practice in early years' settings.

Music and me:
this is only the beginning

Kimberley Birrell

I can't remember when I first began to take an interest in music, but I do know that for as long as I can remember I have been associated with it. At primary school, I learnt to play the recorder when I started Year 3 and joined the recorder group, where I was always praised for doing well. I was proud of myself and what I was achieving, as others appeared to struggle. I quickly learnt to read music and I enjoyed learning to play more and more difficult pieces.

I have been encouraged to pursue music from a young age. When I was 10 I was given the opportunity to learn to play the flute and I fully embraced it. I loved the fact that I was one of a small handful within my primary school who was actually learning to play an instrument. I took every opportunity that I could to perform in front of people, such as in concerts and school assemblies, so that I could show them what I could do. In one concert I even made most of the parents in the audience cry as I played *Somewhere over the rainbow*. At this point I had no fears, but this soon changed.

When I started secondary school I continued to have my flute lessons, but my initial love of playing had started to die away and I felt odd playing an instrument when so few people did. This almost led me to give up playing completely, but my mum put her foot down and told me I had to continue as she had paid for my lessons up until the end of the year. At the time, I was very annoyed and I can imagine that I must have been quite moody for some time afterwards, but now I can't thank her enough.

When I moved into Year 9, the head of music told me that I should be attending the school's Big Band. At first I used every excuse I could think of to avoid going, but eventually, and reluctantly, I went and now I love going to Band as well as the million other musical groups I am part of. At this point, my love of music really began to grow and it still continues today. Throughout the two years of my GCSE Music course, I was introduced to a variety of styles I had never come across before and I loved learning anything new relating to music, including how to compose, as I had never attempted this before. This has continued into my A-level studies and I am always more than happy to go to music lessons.

During my time in the 11–16 school I went through some tough times and music acted as an escape for me, whether it was performing in groups or simply listening to music. I became more nervous and scared of performing and I lost a lot of my self-confidence and self-belief though now, with the help of my music teachers, I am gradually regaining these essential qualities and I am trying as hard as I can to overcome my nerves.

My love and passion for music was influenced and inspired by my secondary school music teachers: Alison Richardson, David Johnstone and Christopher Vernon. Their love and enthusiasm for the subject has inspired and influenced me to want to become a music teacher myself. I have always wanted to be a teacher and after doing work experience within my school's music department, where I got to help out in classes and even teach a class (though that wasn't exactly planned), I know that teaching music is what I want to do. I plan to go to university to get a music degree and then go straight into teaching, as I hope that one day I can be the inspiration for pupils that my secondary school music teachers have been for me.

The cuckoo is a pretty bird—
English identity and the folk tradition

June Boyce-Tillman

In this chapter I will show how my relationship with the English folk tradition has changed and developed in response to the ways in which the tradition itself has been presented over the last 60 years. I will use vignettes from my own experience to interrogate notions of identity, musical roots and bi-musicality, through the metaphor of the cuckoo in the nest of English culture.

The first singing lesson I remember was *My sweetheart come along* sung in a large group on a stage in an all-age school in Maybush in Southampton. I also remember the green Cecil Sharp folk-song book for schools, which included songs like *O no John.* I was puzzled by some of the songs:

> A keeper would a shooting go,
> And under his cloak he carried a bow
> All for to shoot a merry little doe
> Among the leaves so green, O.

> Jackie boy! (Master!) Sing ye well! (Very well!)
> Hey down (Ho down) Derry derry down
> Among the leaves so green, O.

Others were beautiful and again I only came to understand them later:

> I sowed the seeds of love
> I sowed them in the springtime
> Gathered them up in the morning so soon
> While small birds sweetly sing

Later in my life I loved songs like *O Waly, Waly,* talking of different kinds of love. These songs were like parables—you understood them when you needed to. They were very different from the explicit scenes of contemporary television. The knowledge was veiled and revealed itself gradually.

I remember folk-dancing to 78 rpm records in the quadrangle at school; in the summer they often buckled in the heat and would not play. I danced Brighton Camp for the Queen's coronation in a field somewhere in Winchester wearing a red striped dress with others in blue striped dresses and the boys in grey flannel suits.

At Southampton Grammar School for Girls, every week we sang from the *New National Songbook.* This was part of a policy of building the identity of the so-called United Kingdom by means of an equal number of English, Irish, Scots and Welsh songs. They were not all folk-songs; some were composed, like *Come lassies and lads*. It also included *David of the White Rock* and *My love's an arbutus*, which was one of my set pieces for O-level. We sang them beautifully—well-kept girls in a well-kept school.

Privately, I was learning singing and sang in the folk-song class in the competitive music festival. I sang in my best dress with hands clasped in front of me and with a classical tone quality:

> The cuckoo is a pretty bird,
> She singeth as she flies,
> She bringeth us good tidings,
> She telleth us no lies.

We were told that the authentic way to sing folk-songs was unaccompanied; but it was implied that the singing style for the classical song and folk-song were the same. We were taught the folk-songs from books containing musical notation and although we knew the country of origin, no background was given to the folk-songs. The nature of *anon* and *trad* remained hidden.

As I got into choirs as a teenager, I met the arrangements of folk-songs by the likes of Vaughan Williams, such as the exquisite arrangement of *The Turtle Dove*. These were alongside arrangements of Hungarian songs by composers who were also collectors, like Kodály and Bartók. I learned academically about the movement in music history called Nationalism, and that songs were collected from rural communities and used in classical pieces to create a distinctively nationalist style. We learned about England as 'The land without music' (see Blake, 1997) and how the discovery of the folk tradition by the likes of Cecil Sharp and Maud Karpeles gave us a distinctive identity in the hands of Holst and Vaughan Williams. At Christmas I sang Christmas carols from traditional sources. I listened to and loved orchestral arrangements like Vaughan Williams' *Folk-song Suite*.

Sunday after Sunday, I sang folk material recycled by Vaughan Williams for hymn texts in *The English Hymnal*. It contrasted with my folk-songs in school but sounded like them. As a folk-song, the tune known as *Kingsfold* was the vehicle for the story of the notorious Red Barn murder:

> Come all you thoughtless young men, a warning take by me,
> And think upon my unhappy fate to be hanged upon a tree;
> My name is William Corder, to you I do declare,
> I courted Maria Marten, most beautiful and fair.

In *The English Hymnal* the text for the tune is very different:

> I heard the voice of Jesus say, 'Come unto me and rest;
> Lay down, thou weary one, lay down thy head upon my breast.'
> I came to Jesus as I was, so weary, worn, and sad;
> I found in him a resting place, and he has made me glad.

I was becoming aware that there might be a mismatch between classical singing styles and community music-making. In *Village School* (1955), Miss Read describes how the Academy-trained village choirmaster, Mr Annent, saw his standards conflicting with the abilities and experience of the group he was being asked to lead. The two traditions meet uneasily. Our church choir was a bit like Miss Read's, although I could not be part of it because only young boys could be there.

Every Saturday we went to my grandparents in Ashurst—a New Forest Village, so I had some experience of village life. My granddad was the village dance-band pianist, but he wanted me to be better than him—he who could play from memory or by ear whatever his community asked of him. And so I joined the Academy. There seemed little relationship between the two traditions. I was taught faithfulness to a written text. My grandfather was taught faithfulness to the well-being of a group of people every Saturday night who danced to his tunes. He practised on the job each Saturday; I spent at least an hour a day—and later three hours—alone practising.

I read music at St Hugh's College, Oxford, and the curriculum was based on an aristocrat's view of the music of the people. As the syllabus ended at 1900, there was little room even for English Nationalism. Again, there was little attempt at contextualization of anything, and ethnomusicology was nowhere to be seen. By now, I learned nothing orally and saw that as a matter for pride. My life as a musician focused on dots on a page which were often mistaken for the real music.

I came to London in the mid-1960s and studied for a PGCE at the Institute of Education, where I met Michael Lane and Jack Dobbs, editor of *The Oxford School Music Course* (Fiske & Dobbs 1954/70). Here, there were some of the folk-songs that I had learned in school and there were references to the Vaughan Williams pieces. However, Ewan MacColl was now on the radio and we were encouraged to examine the protest movement with songs like:

> I met my love by the gas works wall
> Dreamed a dream by the old canal
> Kissed a girl by the factory wall
> Dirty old town
> Dirty old town

My musical horizons widened. Living near Notting Hill just after the race riots, I heard songs about the greedy landlords of the Rachman era. Ordinary people were now writing songs—they were not old, German, male, deaf or dead, as I had learned in the classical canon. But were these folk-songs, in the same sense as those by *anon* and *trad?* Or were they yet another cuckoo in the folk-song nest?

Sydney Carter, whom I got to know well, sang his protest songs in a pub, using a rough voice somewhere between singing and speaking. Rhythm was free and was governed by the poetry of the song. Pitch was often approximate and often used expressively:

> The devil wore a crucifix.
> 'The Christians, they are right,'
> The devil said, 'so let us burn
> A heretic tonight.'

Even though I had been closely in touch with a Hampshire village from my earliest years, I had developed an image of what Georgina Boyes (1993) called *The Imagined*

Village of sweet country folk singing in the harvest and, above all, happy in their work. Now the image was shattered. The milkmaids were no longer working contentedly and I now realized that the tradition stretched back into history as 'the workers' challenged unjust employers, poor working conditions, and their place in the social hierarchy.

None of my education so far had considered pieces of music as having values within them. Music was, I was taught, value-free; it was disembodied sounds encapsulated fully in a comprehensible notation. I now found out, by experience, of Pierre Bourdieu's (1993) idea of social fields—domains of activity with values linked to power relations. In the folk protest world, I encountered a social field that I had not met before.

The tape recorder was now readily available and 'ordinary people' could compose songs and record them on tape. Notation was not necessary until people wanted to produce songbooks; so like Vaughan Williams before me, I wrote down songs that were conceived orally. I came to Cecil Sharp House and learned folk guitar. I learned the patterns of fingers that produced chords; I worked out my chords by ear. This was a huge shift for me and I still can only play the guitar aurally. I found an increased versatility, and armed with a capo I could tackle most things. I sang *Blowing in the Wind,* in pubs, on ships and in the depths of forests.

I went to folk conferences, I met the Copper family, I heard Shirley Collins sing. Joan Baez and Bob Dylan were in the charts. But something was not right. I vividly remember singing *William Taylor*, a song that I had sung at school, at a folk music conference at Keele University. I knew that it had met with disapproval when someone disdainfully referred to it as 'the version from the Cecil Sharp book for schools'. It had never occurred to me, brought up in the notated tradition, there might be different versions of a song. The variety of versions that characterizes the oral traditions was a new field for me.

I also discovered James Reeves' *The Idiom of the People* (1958) and realized how Cecil Sharp had 'doctored' the songs to make them 'suitable for children'. I found the missing verses of *Oh No John*:

> Madam, may I tie your garter
> Just an inch above your knee?
> If my hand should slip a little farther,
> Would you think it ill of me?

> Chorus: Oh, no John, no John, no John, no.

This was very disconcerting. The folk-song tradition in which I grew up—folk-song annexed by the classical tradition—was no longer accepted in the 'genuine' folk tradition. I had the wrong tone colour in my voice and, more significantly, I could not do the ornamentation. I was now a cuckoo in the nest where I thought I had belonged. Sometimes a pair of birds find they have spent the entire summer nursing an interloper. Is this what I had done or what had been done to me?

I found people decrying the work of the folk-song collectors whom I had revered, because in transcribing songs into a literate form they had killed a tradition that should have continued to be passed on orally. Sharp and his co-workers were seen as fossilizing a tradition and stunting its growth. They were not hallowed preservers, as I had been taught, but pernicious destroyers.

My musical world was turned upside-down. With this came a shift in identity. I thought I was English and that this identity was simple and uncomplex. Now I found out about class wars, trades union disputes, different singing styles, oracy and its possibilities of a variety of versions. There was a freedom there, but I now felt ashamed of the tradition in which I had been brought up. Here was the real music of the real people and I could not belong. I went back to St Hugh's and sang *Oh that greedy landlord* alongside *Music for a while* by Purcell. It did not go down well, but it set a pattern for my later life of trying to bring differing traditions together. Can these diverse systems and their associated values coexist in one nest? Or will one always be antagonistic to the practices and values of the other?

The chorus song also turned my world upside down because the relationship of the composer/performer to the audience becomes much closer than in the classical tradition, where it is formalized into clapping at the end of a piece. In the folk traditions the relationship is much more overt and carried by a wide range of subtle signals often incoherent to the listener outside of the tradition.

I found what Turino (2008) called the 'politics of participation'. I had been brought up in a tradition with a separation between audience and performers — physically, in expertise and in understanding. I found a new concept of musical performance — one concerned with musical participation and experience which are valuable for the processes of personal and social integration that make us whole. My move away from the classical tradition has stayed with me and I have striven to create pieces using the classical style that challenge the so-called 'fourth wall' — compositions in which the audience have to sing, one-woman performances where the audience have to move and dance.

Meanwhile, I was teaching in schools and using the Oxford School Music books. Collections like *The Jolly Herring* (Bentley & Bush, 1990) did include folk material alongside pop and musical material. New song books were appearing with songs like *Dirty Old Town* in them. There was also the pressure of the pop world and the rise of the musical. However, I was still not sure about the teaching of class warfare in an institution like a school which was designed to reinforce the status quo. I once offered the head of a Church of England grammar school a song entitled *One man's hands can't tear a prison down*. I still remember her looking over her glasses and saying: 'But, Miss Boyce, it is an incitement to riot.'

The embarrassment over our colonial history was growing at this time. I had been taught how we brought civilization and culture to far-off lands. But now the negatives of the colonial enterprise were becoming clearer. What I had been taught in school as a good and noble enterprise was now a scurrilous quest for world domination. What could we do to put this right?

Multiculturalism appeared to be the answer to the problem, and I responded by editing collections of material from around the world for the classroom. However, that solution for me was nearly shattered while I was editing one of these collections, *Light the Candles* (Tillman, 1991), drawing on material from ethnic minorities all over the country. A person who helped me a great deal was a librarian in Tooting from the Indian subcontinent; at one point in the project she said, 'Are you going to take our music like you took our land?' I was forced to reconsider my world citizenship. Should I be proud of my own tradition? Could I redeem this by being open to others? But now where did I fit? Had I got the tradition wrong—was I really a cuckoo—a dangerous intervener in world politics?

Perhaps at this time I was, as Gregory Bateson (1972) suggests, using new artistic patterns and forms to articulate the integration of different parts of myself and thus facilitate wholeness. And yet, when I came to composition late in my life, I recognized the contours of the tunes that I wrote were rooted in the *English Hymnal* and Cecil Sharp's collections. Reviewers wrote that they sounded as if we had already heard them; I think that this was because of the deep imbibing of the English folk-songs of my school experience.

By now I had decided to change the values of the classical choir and make it inclusive of everyone. I was hearing the stories of exclusion and the damage it had done to people's sense of identity and self-efficacy. My choirs at the university were going to be inclusive with no auditions. The community choir movement was growing as a direct reaction to the exclusive nature of the classical traditions. But, by this time, world music had colonized school music, and the embarrassment about being English had bitten deep into English culture. The music from Africa, in particular, was closer to the pop traditions and seemed to be more readily accessible than the narrative traditions of English folk-song, while also appearing to reverse the negative effects of colonialism.

I was now becoming aware of what happened to songs as they were passed from one culture to another by means of notation. A New Zealand friend pointed out how a Maori song had been changed almost beyond recognition in its version in notated form in the Silver Burdett (Crook, Reimer & Walker, 1985) course. We could not produce either the tone colours or the rhythms of aboriginal singing. When the songs were reduced to notes on a page the context was lost and important aspects of them were ignored.

I found myself returning to my roots but the same dilemmas still haunted me:

- Oracy and literacy
- Different singing styles
- Class consciousness and conflicts
- Decontextualization

But now I have returned to my original identity: to the wonderful tunes, to the timeless stories of loves and losses, to the power relations within any society and how people negotiate them, to the dilemmas of parents and children and the variety of belief systems by which people have made sense of their lives. I have taken the English folk-songs of my youth and made them my own. I can get closer to the tone colour of the traditional singer, but the ornamentation still escapes me. Even if, as a classical musician singing material from the folk world, I was a cuckoo in the nest, I have integrated my 'cuckooness' into my identity, in the same way as, I guess, every good cuckoo manages to do in some way, as it heralds the arrival of spring.

This chapter is an abridged version of a keynote address given at the Out of This World *conference in May 2011, organized by English Folk Dance & Song Society and University of Winchester.*

References

Bateson, G. (1972) *Steps to an ecology of mind: Collected essays in anthropology, psychiatry, evolution, and epistemology*. Chicago: University Of Chicago Press.

Bentley, R. & Bush, R. (eds.) (1990) *The jolly herring*. London: A & C Black.

Blake, A. (1997) *The land without music: Music culture and society in twentieth century Britain*. Manchester: Manchester University Press.

Bourdieu, P. (1993) *The field of cultural production*. Cambridge: Polity Press.

Boyes, G. (1993) *The imagined village*. Manchester: Manchester University Press.

Crook, E., Reimer, B. & Walker, D.S. (1985) *Silver Burdett music centennial edition*. Morristown, N. J.: Silver Burdett Co.

Fiske, R. & Dobbs, J.P.B. (1954/1970) *The Oxford School Music Books*. Oxford: Oxford University Press.

Miss Read (1955) *The village school*. London: Michael Joseph.

Reeves, J. (1958) *The idiom of the people*. London: Heinemann.

Turino, T. (2008) *Music in social life: the politics of participation*. Chicago: Chicago University Press.

Tillman, J. (1991) *Light the candles*. Cambridge: Cambridge University Press.

The songs quoted are all traditional except *The Devil Wore a Crucifix* by Sydney Carter and *Dirty old Town* by Ewan MacColl.

From Billesley to Bognor: a lifetime of music and music education

Roger Crocker

All mixed up

What on earth was a 'mixed infant'? My school was called Billesley Junior and Mixed Infant School, and I do remember getting mixed up trying to find the outside lavatories. I was also mixed up playing the recorder, and very mixed up in my role as the god Pluto in flowing black cloak, a demi-superman! The real reason for my devotion to things mythological was that I rather fancied Rita Darnley (as Persephone).

Mr Davies, my teacher, had been one of the few pilots who survived the war with appropriate qualifications and experience for working in education. He was 'fast-tracked' into general classroom teaching. I can trace my interest in maths, scientific enquiry, geography, sport and of course singing and music to him. He was the first person to teach me how to make things sound good by leaving notes out—an approach which stood me in good stead for the vast amount of sight-reading and accompaniment I engaged in later.

My mother and father both played the piano and my father sang in a high baritone voice. My Uncle Reg ran a jazz combo called *The Four Aces* who were allegedly rather good. There was no real encouragement from other family members, who said, 'Why don't you work towards getting a *real* job. Music will not get you anywhere and certainly won't pay the bills.'

My mother did not play much after my sister and I were born. She took to seeing that we practised very seriously after buying a shiny brand-new Spencer upright for us. After a few years learning piano with Harry Brenand, an oboist in the BBC Midland Light Orchestra, I played the church organ for the first time at the age of nine at St Mary's Church, Moseley.

Finding my musical feet

My new piano teacher in 1958 was Majorie Hazlehurst, a former pupil of Leonie Gombrich in Oxford, who was a pupil of Leschetizky, who was a pupil of Czerny and in turn Beethoven. She absolutely forbade me to play the church organ as she thought it might damage my 'piano fingers'.

I began to take part in competitive festivals from around 1958. Sadly, the 'feedback' in some of these was rather unpleasant and I am not surprised many children did not return to play again. That was unforgivable and it still is. However, I did become more resolute when the estimable Sidney Harrison told me that 'I would not earn a penny' playing Debussy. I did actually.

I went everywhere from John O'Groats to Land's End. It was a fantastic experience and there were some real high spots where I actually won cups, though frankly I really wanted the money prizes. Unlike many colleagues, I suspect, I found competitive festivals very helpful. Listening to others, playing different instruments and being in touch with a wide range of 'real' musicians were strongly beneficial.

The 'Sherring Phase'

Secondary school was painful from the first day ('sherring' means 'fresh herring', a new boy). Some of the initiation rituals were quite unpleasant. Music on the other hand was magic. Gordon Sill from Manchester University brought music education screaming and shouting into the 20th century. He was well connected, too. I remember to this day a recital given by his contemporary, John McCabe, who was a real inspiration and very modest with it. We did Gilbert and Sullivan a lot, we sang in the Birmingham Town Hall many times, we joined with lots of other schools in large choirs and orchestras, we went on tours . . . oh, and I played for assembly every day. I also helped build an early solid-state electronic church organ for our headmaster, Alan Cholmondeley, an aspiring church organist. The organ was never in tune and I had to tune it manually every morning, which radically improved my aural acuity. It also brought me the closest I have come to certain death when I inadvertently lent on an 800-volt power supply and ended up on the other side of the room.

I was also a keen swimmer because I had become round-shouldered through sitting at the piano for so long, sometimes eight hours on both a Saturday and Sunday, to make up for the four hours a day I was *supposed* to be doing daily in the week. On weekdays I was always at the swimming pool by 7.00 am, back at school by 8.00 am and practising on the Steinway in the hall which I played for assembly at 9.00 am. The exercise and piano playing seemed to work well together. We went all around the country for swimming galas and I was selected to swim backstroke in the English Schools 4x100m medley relay, which we won a few times. This was also the time when I began playing water polo and, disaster of disasters, broke a finger. Fortunately it was put back together again with micro-surgery, but I had to learn to play right-handed with only three fingers and a thumb for six months. Shortly after this I was invited to play with the CBSO in Mendelssohn's *Piano Concerto No. 2* under Hugo Rignold, and the Midland Youth Orchestra under the late James Langley.

While this was a great time for me, another turning point was going to the Wednesday lunchtime recitals given by the City Organist, the indomitable and unique George Thalben-Ball. This was a wonderful cultural experience for me as I ate my sandwiches while listening in amazement to the extemporizations based on ideas and tunes from the audience.

My move to where the streets are paved with gold

I continued my studies at the Royal Academy of Music and spent four happy years there. I was taught piano by Guy Jonson, piano accompaniment by Wilf Parry in the same group as (now Sir) Simon Rattle. I had some success in being the RAM Choir pianist and won a few prizes for piano and piano accompaniment.

I started teaching piano and oboe in Enfield to pay the bills and began to develop an interest in music education. This was the time of the Schools Council and Shirley Williams' Green Paper on education. I read John Paynter and Richard Aston's *Sound and Silence* (1970). This completely dispelled my preconceptions about music teaching and showed me what the music curriculum should really contain, and why music education is fundamental to our very being. I made the decision to take the fork in the road to music education rather than playing, although I have always continued to perform to a high level.

I moved to Reading to do a PGCE and met the illustrious Arnold Bentley. When I arrived for interview it was 'Oh no, another b****y organist and pianist. Don't you play any "real" instruments? If you want to do my course you will have to learn violin and a brass instrument.' I did eventually play the violin for a year and required regular 'therapy' in a pint glass. I also took up the euphonium which also received therapy in a pint glass — the difference was that the brass teacher was usually buying. I loved it and still play occasionally.

Schools and singing projects

My musical pathway now turned to schools in London. My first post was in Ealing Green High School, an amalgamation of Ealing Mead Secondary Modern and Ealing Grammar. Most of my classes, except the O-level ones, had 44 pupils. I had a piano, a pile of 78 rpm records and one or two vinyl ones. To say that I had to make it up as I went along was an understatement, but at least the boys sang and we had some great shows and musicals produced by the legendary and very eccentric J. Allen Benstead in the Ealonian Hall, next to the Ealing Film Studios.

In 1980 I moved to Hounslow as Head of Music at Isleworth and Syon School — another amalgamation. The facilities here were much better: a real music suite with practice rooms, an office and modern hi-fi. The department developed a strong focus on music technology. In one year the music A-level results topped the league tables for all state schools. I also started to teach other subjects, including ICT, RE and sport — it was what you did then to make up for having a deputy in the music department.

The cooperation between that school and the Green School for Girls was superb. We participated in everything from classroom activities to major London concerts and started a combined A-level music course which still runs today. I should pay tribute to Sue Cutler who was the wonderful music teacher in the girls' school, still one of the best I have come across in 40 years. Nothing was too much trouble for her and she helped me considerably in developing ideas for the classroom and maintaining high standards in all aspects of music education.

It was during this time that I became involved in the 'Hounslow Singing Project' led by Jean Carter, who is now Music Adviser in Kensington and Chelsea. Jean was a revelation then, and still is of course. The project was one of the best I have ever come across and pre-dated most of the published schemes we now know and love. All primary teachers, not just music teachers, went through the programme on a three-year rotation, funded by schools and, I think, the local education authority.

National dimensions

In 1992, I spotted an advert for a Music Development Officer in Wandsworth and was intrigued. I was delighted to be appointed with the brief of setting up a Wandsworth Music Service, which is still there today. At this time, funding was extremely difficult to find and I spent a lot of time having to generate my own salary through consultancy and Ofsted inspections.

With the advent of the Labour government in 1997 came the fantastic support for music services which has lasted to the present day. The significance of this was huge: we were able to provide funding for schools, to match-fund programmes of support, purchase instruments and develop music centres.

While in Hounslow I had started to take an interest in national forums in music education and worked with several examining boards, SCAA and Becta. I joined what was then the Music Advisers National Association (later to become NAME). In 2003–2004 I was Chair of NAME and it was a very busy year, with the national conference at the Hilton Docklands and a publication *Ideas in—Music Out* focusing on ICT in Music.

Closer to home . . .

In 2005, the West Sussex Music Adviser post appeared and I was absolutely delighted to be appointed at the rather advanced age of 57. It was clear that there was a very special task to do in taking this already highly-acclaimed music service in a different direction. This is still my current post and what can I say? The challenges today are among the greatest I have had to face. We have to deal with a wholly new set of circumstances, even for an 'outstanding' music service. The fiscal constraints are unbelievable now and there is much uncertainty surrounding the future. A lot of the challenge is to do with 'educating' people with little knowledge of music or music education. This has proved the trickiest issue for me. The average person places fairly low importance on music. Whether that is right or not, I will stick my neck out and say that music education is now significantly better than it was 40 years ago. The challenge is to make the next 50 years better than it is now. Who knows what will happen?

Reference

Paynter, J. & Aston, P. (1970) Sound and Silence. Cambridge: Cambridge University Press.

My musical pathway

Edward Cunningham (aged 14)

I was first interested in making music by many aspects affecting my life as a young child. One of these factors was that I listened to music almost non-stop whenever there was a chance. My parents would listen to Mahler, Beethoven or Mozart symphonies when in the car; I would be introduced to a new choral setting by Howells, Purcell or Byrd while eating dinner; and obviously one could not do without the vintage bands of their time.

My primary school was Lanesborough School in Guildford, Surrey. My parents had chosen this school for its broad range of curricular and extra-curricular activities, as well as its high reputation in the musical arts, and I am extremely thankful that it is also the school from which all boys in the Guildford Cathedral Choir are auditioned and selected. I joined the Cathedral Choir at the age of seven and although, when you first start, there can be some frustrating aspects (the hour long choir practices every morning, the evensongs on weekdays and the seemingly endless services on a Sunday), you soon become far more comfortable in the stalls and really start to enjoy and relish every bit of it. It has been one of the greatest experiences of my life, as I am sure every other chorister in the world will say. I did not realize how much I would miss it until I had to leave. The choir was so professional, fun, and produced some spectacular music, while managing to go on exciting adventures around the world and performing in awe-striking services and concerts, of which more later.

Another factor that influenced me is that I also have an elder brother. Brothers can sometimes be frustrating, tiresome, annoying, but I greatly admire mine (not that these previous common attributes of brothers have never applied to him). I admire him for many reasons, but most of all he has been a great role-model to follow in musical terms. He joined the Cathedral Choir three years previous to my own recruitment and really encouraged me into joining it and I thank him for it. He has also achieved very high standards in all his instruments. In addition he achieved a music scholarship to Winchester College that really inspired in me a certain determination to live up to his achievements. The most important thing to master when becoming a musician is the art of practising, and I was really impelled by his example. I was rewarded last year by also gaining a music scholarship to Winchester College.

I feel there have been many significant events that have affected my musical career so far. As I have already mentioned, I joined the cathedral choir as a probationer at the age of seven, before being made a full chorister at the age of eight. This was a great moment for me, meaning that I was permanently in the choir now until the end of my time in prep school. I have had many great experiences to treasure from my time as chorister: for example, singing at the Royal Maundy and receiving Maundy money from the Queen herself. I have been on two choir tours to Bruges and North

America, the latter being a whole 10 days travelling from New York down through Raleigh, Charlotte and finally to Washington, giving an astonishing number of concerts to welcoming audiences and hosts. I sang a couple of solos on the tour, which really boosted my confidence as a singer. I have also performed in many concerts with well-known musicians and composers, such as John Rutter and Aled Jones. The choir has broadcast many times on the radio and recorded many CDs during the time that I was there. Finally, in my last year as a chorister I became a Senior Chorister.

I currently learn the oboe and the piano, and I still sing. After achieving a distinction in my Grade 6 oboe last term, I am working towards my Grade 7 next term. I had the thrilling experience of playing solo oboe in Bach's *Easter Oratorio* at the beginning of this term in the Baroque Ensemble, at the invitation of and directed by a sixth-form musician, for which I earned a 'Headman's Certificate of Contribution to the School' for a 'wonderful' and 'exquisite' solo in the Adagio. Membership of the College Wind Band has certainly developed my sight-reading skills. At the time of writing this, I am sitting my Grade 6 piano in three days' time. I sing in the junior chapel choir and have decided to broaden my musical education by starting to learn the organ next term. When I am old enough, I aspire to be in the senior chapel choir and also to join Cantores Episcopi, the close harmony Winchester College equivalent of The King's Singers—and to my mind just as good. I am also a member of the College Glee Club—a voluntary choir for pupils, staff, parents and anyone else connected to the school. The highlight of last year was singing Bach's B minor mass in Winchester Cathedral.

There have been many people who have been instrumental in helping me develop musically. To begin with there is Stephen Farr, who was my first choirmaster and who has a particularly dry wit. He helped the choir reach great heights, with the help of the sub-organist David Davies. Katherine Dienes-Williams took over from Mr Farr in January 2008 and was an influential figure in encouraging me to consider applying for a music award to Winchester. She inspires great loyalty among the choristers and is always positive and constructive in her approach to managing the choir. Brian Cotterill, Director of Music at Lanesborough, also encouraged my endeavours throughout my time at the school and I am immensely grateful to him for his inspirational teaching. I am also very thankful to all my instrumental teachers throughout my career, but a special mention must go to Joanna Lees, my first oboe teacher, with her inspiring teaching of technique and perfectionism.

Now I am at Winchester, the musical opportunities are endless, with the best support and teaching anyone could wish for. Finally, I could not finish without saying a word about my parents and how grateful I am to them for playing that Mahler, Beethoven, or Mozart when we were in the car, or that motet while eating dinner. Without them I would definitely not be the musician I am today, through the encouragement they have given me to pursue my instrumental interests, or the many hours of driving time to and from lessons.

That has been my musical pathway so far, but this journey has not ended, it has only just begun.

Pensions to pedagogy: a musical journey

James Garnett

'Oh, it's you!' These were the words of my son, then aged three, when I woke him up one Friday morning, not having seen him since the previous Sunday night. They were the catalyst that accelerated my growing dissatisfaction with life as a well-paid (and overworked) management consultant in the pensions industry. A few weeks later, our expensive house was on the market, my application for a secondary PGCE was submitted and I had made one of the best decisions of my life.

I had joined Coopers & Lybrand (as it was then — it later became PricewaterhouseCoopers) as a trainee actuary after completing my DPhil on music theory and aesthetics at St Hugh's College, Oxford. Quite how I got this job I still don't understand. It was a triumph of transferable skills, as most actuaries are maths graduates (the exceptions being statisticians) and my A-level pure maths was a long time ago. I never qualified as an actuary, but I did discover a love of computers and an interest (yes!) in pensions, enabling me to carve out a profitable and enjoyable niche for myself that developed over seven years.

During this time I retained my contact with music as a church organist. I had taken up the organ properly when I went to study music at Exeter University. Previously, I had received some lessons (initially from my mother) when I was about 10, following an early obsession with the instrument, but had been persuaded to put my studies on hold until I had gained a grounding in piano technique. Piano lessons started with my father, who taught me to play boogie-woogie. This gave me a taste for improvisation before I got anywhere near technique. In addition, playing through the songs and piano pieces Dad had composed while a member of the Entertainments Society at Nottingham University persuaded me that I might also be able to write music. I was 15 when I started formal piano lessons, although by this time I had been learning the violin for six years or so. Thanks to Mum's persistence I had learned the habits of practice by then (and again thanks to her had learned to read music before I started school), so I progressed quickly, taking Grade 8 on both piano and violin while in the Sixth Form. It was also in the Sixth Form that I began to flourish as a composer. I had received great encouragement at my secondary school from Rosemary Williams, the head of music, who had studied with Alun Hoddinott at Cardiff University. This developed further at Farnborough Sixth Form College, partly because I had a girlfriend who wrote poems (which invited setting to music, naturally) and partly because Peter Mound, the head of music, challenged me to engage with contemporary music as well as giving me opportunities such as having a composition performed by the Area Youth Orchestra.

I arrived, then, at Exeter, a half-decent pianist, a slightly better violin player and an aspiring composer. I emerged three years later as a slightly accident-prone organist, a reliable viola player and an aspiring academic. I was, I suspect, a sore disappointment to my organ teacher, Paul Morgan, who also taught keyboard harmony in the music department. Although my boogie-woogie piano skills transferred successfully to improvising from a figured bass, and my composing enabled me to harmonize a melody at sight, I could not co-ordinate my limbs at the organ console—despite hours of practice. This combined with the discovery of Schenker's music theory and Adorno's aesthetics, under the guidance of Jim Samson, to edge me away from practical music-making towards the interests that I followed up in my DPhil. These were to do with complexity in music—the way that music theory always falls short of its ambitions to explain musical practice and labels this shortfall as 'complexity'. Life in a library did not suit me well, however. I very nearly left Oxford after the first term, but decided that the DPhil was something I had to get out of my system. So it was that I knuckled down, completed my thesis in three years and then shook the dust of music and academia off my feet to train as an actuary with Coopers & Lybrand.

Seven years of playing hymns and psalms every weekend while calculating pensions during the week sorted out my co-ordination problems, but also rekindled an awareness of just how important music was to me. Not only did I find myself looking forward to my own retirement so that I could do some more music again, but I found myself looking for a more worthwhile purpose in life than making myself (and my employers) rich. (All those sermons must have had an effect.) These were the ingredients that my son's words brought together. Having positively not wanted to teach music while at Exeter, this route now emerged as the ideal way of addressing my social conscience whilst re-engaging with the musical activity that I had gradually come to take for granted during my years of full-time study.

So, the house sold, I handed in my notice and started my PGCE at Reading University in 2000 (this is the course that I now lead). This was an amazing year in which I reconnected with musical skills I had forgotten I possessed, acquired new ones I didn't know existed and was constantly challenged musically, intellectually and emotionally. The skills that I rediscovered were composing and improvising. I became rather self-conscious at university and found myself thinking about it too much to be able to express myself. The PGCE, however, gave a definite purpose to my attempts, and I found that the ability to improvise and to develop improvisations into compositions emerged as the most important element of my teaching. It enabled me to hear the implications of students' music and to help them to think them through, as well as encouraging me to think of established musical works from a creative point of view. Amongst the new skills that I developed in my PGCE year, the most significant was drumming. How to assemble a drum kit was one piece of knowledge I learned that year that I used practically every day for the following seven, enabling me to piece back together again the kits that students had strewn across numerous practice rooms. Having assembled the kit, the ability to play a few simple patterns proved to be a very useful way of holding the attention of a class (even if it did challenge afresh my ability to co-ordinate my limbs). Perhaps the most lasting impression of the year, however, and one that I share with each cohort of my own PGCE students, was the feeling during teaching practice of starting the day with at least one thing that I didn't think I would be capable of doing and getting to the end of the day somehow having achieved it.

I spent my NQT year learning a great deal in a boys' comprehensive school, then became head of department (thanks to my management experience with PricewaterhouseCoopers) in the school where I had completed my teaching practice. The best thing about this job was my colleagues, one of whom was immensely experienced and had mentored me on my PGCE, and the other a brilliant NQT (from the Reading PGCE course). Our teamwork was built on the recognition that we each had different strengths and that we wanted to learn from each other in order to extend what we could do. My priority was to find out about music technology — which hadn't been invented when I was studying music. I had devoted the last three weeks of my PGCE to finding my way around a mixing desk, and that gave me a head start as I endeavoured to learn A-level music technology a few weeks ahead of the students.

It was a student in this school who studied both A-level music and music technology who has perhaps taught me most about music and how it is learned. He was a brilliant jazz drummer as well as a Grade 8 cellist. Not only did he open my ears to the intricacy of rhythm in jazz, but the way in which he assimilated music from a vast range of listening, and distilled characteristics of it in his composition and recording work really grounded me in what it is to think and learn musically.

Continuing to learn about teaching is the most rewarding aspect of my job at Reading. Planning and leading sessions for the PGCE and GTP students, responding to their individual progress and reading more widely constantly challenges my understanding of teaching music and of how to learn how to do it. The one disadvantage of the job is the lack of contact with young people's music-making, and I try to arrange at least one activity each year that keeps me in touch. For two years, this involved running a choir at a Young Offenders Institute — with the aid of two PGCE students in the second year. This was another milestone in my development as a teacher. Not only did it challenge my application of singing technique (we did end up with a tuneful rendition of both *Lean on me* and Joubert's *Torches!*), but it also forced me to develop positive, pre-emptive behaviour management (there was no telling them to stand outside the door after they had misbehaved).

When I started to write this, my impression was that my path into music education was a twisted one. On reflection, I see a series of straight sections of several different paths, linked by unmarked journeys through the undergrowth as I have changed route. As I contemplate my year ahead as Chair of NAME, I become acutely aware of my debt to those who laid the paths that I have trodden and tended them to keep them in good repair and clear of brambles. I am also aware of those who have guided and encouraged me along the paths, teaching me so that I would be able to read the map for myself and have the confidence to dive off into the undergrowth to find my own route. This is the challenge and the responsibility that music educators currently face — perhaps more in the coming years than for quite some time. We need to keep in good condition the paths that have served us well and brought us to where we are. At the same time we need to recognize that new routes are needed in a world — a musical world — that changes constantly. Yet, perhaps above all, it is in our role as guides that we are needed most, not least because we gain so much from those who travel with us.

Pathway to percussion

Evelyn Glennie

As a child I was lucky in many ways to live on a farm north of Aberdeen. My upbringing was very much concerned with the functions of a busy working farm and involved a great deal of understanding and respect for the environment, family and neighbours.

Respect for others was instilled in me from a very early age. I was educated locally at Cairnorrie Primary School where the older pupils helped with the younger ones and as they in turn grew they took over the role of peers to the next intake. Later, at Ellon Academy, the school policy was about inclusion and opportunity for all.

My observations today are that we live in a much more insular way. Our home entertainment includes television, DVD, radio, CD and computer-game entertainment which can mean limited interaction within the family. I know many families who spend evenings, weekends and most meals in separate rooms in pursuit of individual entertainment. This seems very alien from my own upbringing and I wonder if the casualty is social inclusion.

Living on a farm meant that there were numerous chores that were shared between my two brothers and me. The completion of these chores instilled a tremendous sense of responsibility into us and as a consequence I felt we all grew up as well rounded individuals.

At Ellon Academy I had already begun to lose my hearing and the realization that there might be possible limitations was slowly dawning on me. My hopes of a career in music became tenuous until our music teacher, Ron Forbes, introduced me to percussion. At that time the Academy had its own orchestra ensembles. I viewed the options and saw that percussion had enormous scope, not least because of the sheer number of instruments in the percussion section, which later encouraged me to begin my own personal collection of percussion instruments. That week my teacher sent me home with a snare drum—no sticks, no mallets, just the drum. I thought this was wonderful, at first. But then I thought, what do I do with this? The drum was placed around the farmhouse, on floors, grass, bales, bed—you name it. I placed that drum on as many surfaces as I could find. I tapped, scraped, banged and stroked the head and the sides—in fact I explored every surface of that drum, turning the snares on and off. I can still envisage how it felt even now.

Back at school my teacher asked how I had got on—I wasn't sure what he meant. So he asked me to create the sound of rain, snow, wind and I demonstrated my interpretation of each element using the surfaces of the snare drum—still no sticks.

Ron Forbes demonstrated a high level of patience and believed passionately that everyone should be given the same opportunities and our curiosity should be encouraged, especially in music. This has remained with me all my life. He also instilled in me that first and foremost I was a sound creator, and thereafter I learned to become a musician and an interpreter of music.

I was, however, in for a bit of a shock at the Royal Academy of Music in London, where the institute was stuck and staid in its approach to students with hearing loss. I presented them with a dilemma and it was difficult for them to see how I could possibly fit into their 'system'. They could not envisage teaching music to a deaf person. With support from my family and from Ann Rachlin of the Beethoven Fund for Deaf Children, I was eventually able to persuade the Academy to open its doors to me. The next issue was the fact that I had always dreamed of becoming a solo percussionist. However, I had not realized that this role simply did not exist at the time and furthermore there was very little music written for solo percussion either.

At this point my stubbornness and self belief came to the fore and I set about persuading a fellow student to write something for me to perform for an exam. From there I embarked on a lifetime practice of encouraging composers to write pieces for solo percussion and orchestras to perform them. This was essential for the career I was carving out for myself, and to date I have commissioned almost 170 new works.

My early education was standing me in good stead and my determination was finding a strong footing. Throughout my career I have found ways to share my passion for percussion not only with audiences but with conductors, composers, orchestras, a host of great collaborators and thousands of fans worldwide.

Bringing percussion to the front of the stage has been an enormous struggle at times — not only physically but mentally too. Overcoming barriers, stigmas and mindsets in order to perform with the best has been a very interesting journey and I have enjoyed the many friendships which have arisen from so many kind and generous people.

Transporting instruments was another major hurdle which came to a full stop when the USA suffered the 9/11 attacks. Security issues became paramount and taking a nine foot by five foot marimba together with a whole gamut of other strange looking instruments became too difficult. Nowadays orchestras and organizers are extremely accommodating and we get round the problem by hiring instruments for each event.

I have found the role of solo percussionist has led to many interesting avenues and opportunities, including the production of my own ranges of jewellery with a percussion theme. I have also climbed Mount Kilimanjaro through my work with Able Child Africa and I am looking forward to revisiting Africa to meet some of the children who will benefit from the money the charity has raised towards their education.

My understanding of the body and how it receives vibration has proved to be extremely beneficial and I am now able to share my experiences with others around the globe including the corporate industries. I am often asked whether, if I could turn back the clock, I would choose to do anything differently. I can honestly say no. I had the best chances because of my family, teachers and social groups and I am fully aware that my chosen pathway would not have happened without them.

More by accident than design

Richard Hallam

I have never thought of myself as ambitious, and yet, from a very ordinary background you could be forgiven for thinking that to have an MBE, advised Government ministers and influenced national policy for music education, there must have been some great scheme, a lot of drive, determination and aspiration. Nothing could be further from the truth. My musical pathways came about more by accident than design. They were shaped by the music, by friendships and by out of school experiences in various communities.

My primary school music education was not particularly memorable. My parents were not especially musical. They were supportive and encouraging and, as regular chapel-goers, they encouraged me to sing in the church concert party and at Sunday school.

I started playing the cornet in the local brass band because, at around the age of 9, my friend Ken wanted to join and I went along with him. My memory of my first lesson was being given a cornet and shown how to 'buzz', and then being given the fingering for the scale of C major (notated in semibreves on a scrap of manuscript paper) and told to come back next week able to play it. Hymn tunes followed, with additional notes and rhythms introduced as and when needed for me to play third and then second cornet in the band. I must have had some aptitude as I survived this sink or swim approach and graduated over time to become solo cornet. Christmases were marked by carols in the community, raising funds for the band. Then there was the *Last Post* on Remembrance Sunday and various parades in the surrounding area.

My primary school head teacher told my parents that I ought to join the Leicestershire School of Music on Saturday mornings. My parents couldn't afford to buy me a trumpet, but a neighbour had one in the attic, which was duly dusted down and loaned to me. Someone else said I ought to learn the piano, so Ken's grandma offered to teach me and another neighbour allowed me to practise on her piano.

My parents' values and beliefs meant that, as I became more involved with the School of Music, I continued to support the local band and, in turn, helped to teach the new junior members. Similarly, I learned from others: Eric Pinkett, who was then in charge in Leicestershire, strongly believed in older students acting as mentors. I remember, still wearing short trousers, playing sixth trumpet in Malcolm Arnold's *Divertimento* being supported by Bruce Johnson, Maxi Stamford, Diane Henderson and John Betteridge—so who was that fifth person? Was it Colin or Steve? Sorry, I really can't remember, although I do recall the phenomenal Jimmy Watson coming along a few years later and being part of the same section.

Much as I loved the sound of the brass band and benefited technically from those incredibly challenging arrangements, I also loved the sound of the orchestra and the great music that I was introduced to.

People talk about *El Sistema*, but for me and many of my contemporaries, the Leicestershire Schools Symphony Orchestra in the 1960s served exactly the same purpose. My musical friends became my second family and music took up almost all of my spare time. Pinkett knew that, by introducing us to demanding music of high quality, by giving us a sense of pride and lots of performance opportunities, we would rise to the challenge. He was also selfless, rehearsing us himself, then bringing in people like Norman del Mar and Malcolm Arnold to conduct our concerts and recordings. I was a member when Michael Tippett first became involved in the orchestra, and from Rudolph Schwartz I learned that you don't play at your best if you are terrified of the conductor.

Technically I continued to learn in response to the musical demands of the repertoire. I learned to double tongue because we played Britten's *Young Person's Guide to the Orchestra*; I learned to triple tongue for *Karelia Suite*; I learned to transpose when we played Beethoven's *Fifth*.

For many years my teacher was Bert Neale, a former military band clarinettist who taught woodwind and brass at my secondary school in one room, all at the same time. We would be given more scraps of manuscript with challenging snippets of music, often related to something we were playing in the orchestra (Bert was also the wind coach on Saturday mornings) while Bert was fixing a pad on a flute or hearing someone else play. We were terrified of Bert, but not in the same way as Schwartz. The difference was that somehow we knew Bert wanted us to succeed and to have confidence. Bert had great musicianship, understood how to motivate young people and had sufficient technical knowledge to support us on our journey.

Lessons were at lunchtime, which stopped me playing football with my peers. This, and not being available for the school team on Saturday mornings because of the orchestra, caused me to suffer much pressure from my school friends to give up music. But when, at the age of 13, I went with the orchestra to Sweden, without my parents, being a member of the orchestra suddenly had street credibility. Those concert tours and the intense Easter residential courses when we slept on camp beds in school classrooms also brought a very special social element to being in the orchestra. Our responsibility to the younger students was there too: senior students went along to the 'intermediate orchestra' courses and helped the younger members with repertoire that would otherwise have been beyond their technical ability.

My piano playing was functional. I was told that I needed Grade 6 so my teacher took me from one grade to the next. I passed my exams, but the only pieces of Grade 6 standard that I could play were those I had to learn for the exam. On the other hand, I did not take any exams on the trumpet until I got to the Royal Academy.

My school music lessons consisted of singing and listening to records. I learned to harmonize mathematically, applying rules like the leading note must rise and avoid consecutive fifths. My secondary music teacher was encouraging and supportive of the School of Music, also giving me the opportunity to play my first concerto with the school orchestra. By the age of 15, music was so obviously my life that going to a conservatoire was almost a foregone conclusion, so Pinkett arranged for me to have lessons with the late, great Ernest Hall. About once a fortnight I would travel to his home in Lewisham for my hour-long lessons.

I decided to go to the Royal Academy of Music and was fortunate to be taught by Sidney Ellison. I must have been quite good as Sidney successfully entered me for my first trumpet exam in my first year: an external LGSM. I went on to be awarded a Certificate of Merit for trumpet playing and performed the Vivaldi double trumpet concerto on tour in Jersey with the Academy chamber orchestra. I will be eternally grateful to Sidney for taking me on gigs with him to get professional experience, and for teaching me to become an independent learner, to analyse the sound I wanted to make and to explore how to get it.

I have already touched upon the importance of repertoire, but it is worth mentioning that Pinkett introduced us to modern works as well as the greats. In particular I remember Rawsthorne and Ridout and bars that contained 7 + 5 over 16 which later resulted in my being completely unfazed when sight-reading Stravinsky's *Rite of Spring*. We got through enormous amounts of repertoire, thrown at us with the expectation that we would play the music to a high standard. There was never time to be bored. We worked hard, not wanting to let each other down.

Whilst these experiences resulted in me becoming a great reader it was not all good. I knew little of improvising, playing by ear or other styles. Fortunately, my reading ability helped me to get work. People like saxophonist Tony Carter wrote out 'improvised' solos for me and Ray Farr introduced me to jazz quavers. Later, this is why I became so passionate about young musicians needing to learn to play by ear and improvise *as well as* developing excellent reading skills.

I have spent a long time writing here about my formative years. I didn't realize at the time that they were not typical. But with hindsight I can see how much they influenced my views on music education, my values and my passion for bringing these and better opportunities to young people everywhere.

Pinkett said he wouldn't give me a fourth year grant to stay on at the Academy but would fund me to go to Trent Park to get my PGCE. Like many young players, I had no intention of teaching, but it did help to pay the rent.

The next 15 years were wonderful. I was fortunate to play many of the greatest works with brilliant conductors and fabulous musicians. I became assistant MD at the Birmingham Hippodrome. My ability to double tongue resulted in Gene Pitney asking me to play whenever he toured in the UK. (Those of you who recall *24 Hours from Tulsa* will know what I mean). My ability to read at sight and to transpose resulted in me becoming 'first call extra' with the CBSO after playing second cornet in *Francesca di Rimini* without rehearsal under Louis Fremaux.

Nevertheless, by my mid 30s I was asking myself if this was what I wanted to do for the next 30 years. A teaching job came up, which still allowed me to play, so I took it. My teaching experiences ranged from schools in the most deprived parts of West Bromwich to independent schools. But a lack of intellectual stimulation led to me taking an Open University degree including credits in modelling in mathematics; computers and computing; and various management courses. There was no plan. These just interested me. But later, when I became a music adviser and the head of music service in Oxfordshire, they were invaluable.

The more I became involved in education, the harder it was to keep my playing up to the same standard. The day I realized that I had to concentrate not on the music, but physically on what I was doing to ensure I played to a professional standard, was the day I decided to stop. I couldn't imagine life without practical music-making so I focused more on conducting the youth orchestra. I wanted to empower the young people to discover the music in them. I wanted to give them confidence and self-esteem. But it was more than the music. Our mantra was 'consideration for others' and 'personal responsibility'.

So how have these influences helped my ideas to develop?

As recognized by both the Music Manifesto (DfES/DCMS, 2004) and the Henley Report (2011), music education takes place in and out of school, formally and informally. None of us do it alone. All professional musicians should have some basic grounding in education. Older students benefit others and themselves by helping their younger peers. We all need networks of people who are ready to help; to provide the signposts to different pathways and the resources needed for the musical journey. Everyone should have access to appropriate opportunities, support and guidance. Friendships and peer groups are significant factors in learning, and I suspect this is why I see no tension between the importance of good music education in its own right and the personal and social benefits that music can bring.

All of these experiences emphasized for me the importance to learning of relevance and purpose. Used well, examinations can be a great motivator, but should not be ends in themselves. Repertoire is so important. Great music, ensemble playing and performance, with suitable challenges, enable young people to exceed our (and their) expectations.

I stayed in Oxfordshire for over 25 years because there was always more I wanted to achieve. I had a great staff and we undertook a fabulous journey together. I consider myself to have been enormously lucky with the opportunities that have come my way and with the people I have worked with. What they have taught me is that it is the people and the music that matter.

References

DfES/DCMS (2004) *The Music Manifesto*. London: DfES/DCMS

Henley, D. (2011) *Music Education in England*. London: Department for Education

Career paths:
a Grand Union Orchestra perspective

Tony Haynes

Early days

I invented my first piece of music on my grandma's parlour piano around the age of six, and at that point knew I would be a composer.

I spent most of my childhood and teenage years in a country town in the north of Berkshire, where I had piano lessons with stern Mrs Lambert, sang in the choir (and later played the organ) in the local church and joined a couple of brass bands to acquire a trombone. From the age of 13—as National Service was claiming the more experienced semi-pro musicians—I would play most Friday nights and Saturdays in local bands for dances and weddings across the Berkshire downs; and then I discovered jazz and blues as the New Orleans revival took off.

At school I took up the viola, taught by the inspirational Frances Kitching, who gave me opportunities I didn't deserve, given my technical shortcomings and reluctance to practise; she nurtured me and gave me unstinting encouragement and criticism until she died tragically young. I also directed our cadet force band and organized various jazz groups. In music theory I was entirely self-taught, and passed O-level and A-level Music without formal teaching. I scraped into Oxford via a classics scholarship, but was offered a place on condition I study something else. I readily opted for music.

I relished the highly academic discipline of the Oxford music degree in those days, loved writing fugues and five-part counterpoint, and took twelve-tone music as a special subject in Finals, with Egon Wellesz—a real composer, pupil of Schönberg—as my tutor. Two close friends and I ran the popular and well-off University Jazz Club in our final year. We lived in an enormous house in North Oxford where famous musicians (and often whole bands) up from London could be tempted with a bottle of whisky or two to jam into the night with us student musicians; by this stage I was playing modern jazz piano rather than trad trombone. I emerged that summer with a respectable BA class 2:1.

Needing a complete change of direction, I signed up with an agency in Paris that provided bands for American Air Force bases in France and for several months played under a succession of German band-leaders in Enlisted Men's and Officers' Clubs from Normandy to Verdun. I was playing in one of these when Kennedy was assassinated, the work collapsed, and I was home for Christmas. The following summer I spent with my trio, a charming Brazilian singer/guitarist called Bira and a student fado group from Lisbon opening one of the first night clubs in the Algarve; shortly after, I settled in London.

After three years of varied freelance work, teaching and part-time study I signed up for a brand new MA course at Nottingham University in the Analysis of Contemporary Music. Here I discovered Messiaen, but my dissertation was actually in indeterminacy and aleatoric music, in particular Lutosławski and Penderecki. During my year at the university I played in a couple of productions at the Playhouse (the MD at that time happened to be an old Oxford music acquaintance), and this led to perhaps the greatest stroke of luck in my entire career . . .

Luck and opportunity

It is generally said that you make your own luck, but taking every opportunity that's offered—however apprehensive (or unqualified) you may feel—is essential to the development of any musician or creative artist. You never know where it may lead: there is the occasional blind alley, but there is scarcely any experience from which you don't learn something valuable. Up to this point, I had passed up perhaps two or three significant opportunities—including one I still deeply regret—and it wasn't going to happen again.

So I became Musical Director at Nottingham Playhouse—the only salaried job I've had in an otherwise self-employed career—with only limited experience of theatre, but it was the ideal job. It provided me with a chance to use all my strongest compositional skills, and develop others (including management and negotiation, as well as directing and performing). The theatre at that time ran productions in repertoire, so that in any one week there would be two or three different shows. Most of these shows would contain live music, and all that music I would write or arrange; occasionally it would be recorded, and I could spend hours cutting up and playing around with tape.

For the next 10 years, writing and directing my own music for theatre was my life (although most Mondays for five years I also taught harmony and degree students at Trinity College of Music). Reputations spread quickly then, and I was in great demand—for four years I contributed to all Alan Dossor's legendary productions at the Liverpool Everyman, I worked in Newcastle, Leicester (Haymarket and Phoenix), Birmingham and with the RSC, where *The Taming of the Shrew* gained a SWET (Society of West End Theatre) award. I diversified into dance (Ludus in Lancaster) and perhaps most importantly joined the touring companies 7:84 and Belt & Braces Roadshow. Many of these productions would be called 'political theatre', which shaped a lot of my subsequent thinking; besides writing music for plays by people like John Arden, John McGrath and Chris Bond, I wrote new music for many Brecht productions, and his ideas about theatre deeply influenced much of my own subsequent work. The network of collaborators, venues and promoters I built up during years of touring was also invaluable.

It was therefore time to put these ideas into practice on my own account—creating work not dependent on a script and actors, putting music at the centre, with other performance disciplines in an ancillary role—so David Bradford, John Cumming, Julie Eaglen and I formed our own company: Grand Union was born with our first touring show Jelly Roll Soul.

Other journeys

Among the many factors that make Grand Union successful and give it its unique identity, one of the most significant is 'authenticity'. This is difficult to define and express—like the parallel concept of 'artistic truth', which is equally important—but you know it when you experience it. Perhaps the best way is to give an example.

Our third touring show was Strange Migration, performed by eight multi-instrumentalists/singers. I had long wanted to produce a piece exploring aspects of migration and realized it would be dishonest (thank you, Bertolt!) unless some of the performers themselves had this experience. Among the performers I recruited were Sarah Laryea, who might be described as an economic migrant, and Vladimir Vega, a political exile.

Sarah had come to England from Ghana a few years before to join Steel An' Skin, which memorably pioneered a combination of Caribbean and West African music and dance. A charismatic drummer, singer and dancer—born into a long-established family of master-drummers—she brought to Grand Union Ghanaian songs and West African drum rhythms that formed the bedrock of much of our early repertoire and workshop practice. (Whenever we perform them, even today, they are always led by an African or African-descended musician.) It turned out later that Sarah had never played drums in public before she joined Grand Union, as this is regarded as the men's prerogative in Ghana. Everything she knew, and played with supreme confidence, she reproduced from what she had heard for years as a dancer, from the rhythms of the drum ensemble accompanying her.

Vladimir had been a student agitator, and after President Allende was overthrown and assassinated, he was among thousands rounded up and thrown into prison, and narrowly escaped being 'disappeared'. He didn't regard himself at that point as a musician, but music had already radicalized many young people and had, in turn, become politicized in Chile, so for many in gaol it formed a focus of resistance, a way of preserving morale—and quite simply passing the time. So Vladimir learnt (and made) traditional instruments like the charango, kena and pan-pipes, acquired an enormous repertoire of traditional Andean music from his fellow inmates, and began writing his own deeply personal and political songs. Following the amnesty that brought him and so many Chileans to Britain, this knowledge and practice laid the foundations for his professional musical career.

The 'stories' of Sarah, Vladimir and other migrants, exiles and refugees were written into Strange Migration (which toured the UK for over a year)—and into many subsequent Grand Union Orchestra shows—through a quite subtle and complex collaborative process. It's one reason why the work always packs such an emotional punch. But the range of purely musical expertise brought by these and other musicians is equally important. Mostly born outside the UK, often making a quite precarious living, their careers have been shaped first by the traditions in which they were brought up, and then by the experience of settling, living and working in Britain; and, of course, their music and musical identity have been transformed accordingly. Their career paths would make fascinating and instructive reading analysed in detail; here are some very brief summaries:

Zhu Xiao Meng first played piano as a child, then trained in the Chinese music school of Shanghai, where she became a featured gu zheng soloist in the traditional orchestra.

Yousuf Ali Khan ran away to Kolkata as a 12-year-old to learn tabla, and—by a chance meeting in Kolkata airport—was recruited at 22 by Peter Fletcher as a founder-member of the epoch-making South Asian music school set up by Leicester City Council.

Lucy Rahman was taught by her father, a famous Bengali classical singer and writer of protest songs in support of Bangladesh independence.

Baluji Shrivastav was identified as a talented musician at an early age and learnt sitar and the rudiments of Hindustani music in a special school for blind children in Agra.

Paul Jayasinha was born in England to a Sri Lankan father and Scottish mother, learnt cello and trumpet, studied computer sciences at Cambridge, became a fine jazz player and is in the process of discovering the culture of his South Asian roots;

Cemal Akkiraz, from a distinguished dynasty of Anatolian singers and baglama players, was a political refugee from his native Turkey, and established the first (independent) school for saz players in North London.

Claude Deppa, drummer as well as jazz trumpeter, was already a featured cornet player in his grandfather's well-known brass band when he left South Africa for London with his family aged 12.

Brian Abrahams, classified as 'Cape Coloured', began as a teenage crooner in function bands, listened to his father's Duke Ellington 78s and became an acclaimed jazz drummer, sought-after sideman to many touring American artists.

Ken Johnson, extraordinary pan player, acquired a very sophisticated knowledge of harmony, plays bebop and wonderfully lyrical solos, travelled the world as a young musician and is at home in virtually any genre.

Carlos Fuentes, another Chilean refugee, escaped from Chile over the mountains, came to Britain via Brazil, acquiring a deep love and knowledge of Brazilian music.

My Journey as a composer

Traditional material or 'standards' from different musical cultures around the world form part of the Grand Union repertoire, but the music for the Grand Union Orchestra or our large-scale participatory shows is my own. I couldn't have written it, however, without working with and learning from all the musicians—and more—listed above. Establishing and developing the Grand Union Orchestra has therefore been by far the most significant factor in my own career.

First, everything I know about 'world music' comes from the musicians I work with, not from books, records or ethno-musicological study. They are themselves very resourceful, happy to share their musical knowledge and insights and learn from musicians from other disciplines; all are creative, and confident improvisers whatever their tradition.

The best way to get under the skin of musicians you work with—if you want to write something original and effective for them to perform—is to learn as much as you can about the music they are familiar with, that they regularly perform. So, Baluji may suggest an Indian raga which may generate some unusual harmonies, or Claude will talk me through some African rhythms as the basis of a big brass/sax ensemble, and the resulting material will then feature their particular skills.

It's similar writing for voices. I long ago realized that the vocal and emotional characteristics I admire in 'world' singers tend to disappear with lyrics in English—you need to write in their language. While setting Portuguese or Spanish is relatively easy, I also have to write in languages I scarcely understand, and certainly cannot speak; so to set Bengali I need Lucy's patient guidance on all her vocal inflections, while Wei Li has to demonstrate the way individual syllables in Chinese are pitched, or must rise and fall.

While the content of a song, or indeed a whole show, may express directly the experience of those performing it, even instrumental music can be written in such a way that improvising soloists, for example (like Claude or Baluji described above), have an appropriate vehicle in which to express their musical personalities. Composition is not just the manipulation of notes, but the expression of a powerful artistic idea through the most appropriate and effective means available, driven by creative purpose.

These are all also aspects of the 'authenticity' integral to Grand Union's work, and the work belongs jointly to all of us.

Career paths for young musicians

Opportunity is the key to artistic development, and young musicians deserve the kind of opportunities I and other Grand Union musicians have had. However, lessons are best learnt in the real world associating with practical, professional musicians from diverse backgrounds, rather than only through colleges, conservatoires, training and leadership courses—and, sadly, such opportunities have been steadily declining for years.

Offering effective, meaningful and varied career paths to young musicians, and giving them the creative opportunities they need to develop their own musical personality, depends on many factors—social stability and mobility, open-minded educationists, enlightened funders, and above all a healthy live music scene. They also need to know the many (often unfashionable, but exhilarating) directions music-making may take: this is best done by demonstration, and the chance to participate in a range of practical workshop activities culminating in performance.

Grand Union's own Youth Orchestra—open to any young musician who plays a non-western instrument, or western instrumentalists who want to learn more about world music—exemplifies this. It gives regular, often high-profile, public performances prepared through a programme of monthly masterclasses by our diverse roster of core musicians. And out of this is emerging 'Grand Union—the Second Generation', a new and exciting group of British-born musicians who, given encouragement and opportunity, will find creative ways of combining their own experience of growing up in the UK with the musical traditions of their grandparents.

To demonstrate in practice some of the composition techniques he has developed over years with the Grand Union Orchestra, Tony Haynes has recently started a musical blog accessible through the GUO website www.grandunion.org.uk, or directly at www.tonyhaynesmusic.wordpress.com

Learning on the job

Jan Holdstock

I gave up the piano at the age of seven. My parents had been passing me from one to the other, muttering, 'I can't make anything of her, you have a try.' Finally, in desperation, I was given a quarter-sized violin. Looking back, I can see their teaching strategy. Neither of them could play the violin, so I had something of my own. Also, probably to avoid listening to my playing out of tune, my mother, who had perfect pitch, used to accompany my practice. That was fun, but there were high expectations too. No playing wrong notes and no getting the rhythm wrong either. Both my parents (Lionel and Freda Nutley) were music teachers. My father went on to be a music adviser in Cumberland and my mother taught teachers at Alnwick College. They worked very well as a double-act. In those days, children played percussion from big charts with simple, coloured notation. My parents used to go around the local Women's Institutes with a big box of percussion and the ladies used to bang the drums happily while my mother played the piano. My father had a wonderful way with these ladies and I was wheeled out to play my violin, to have my head patted, and to be given cake.

The music at Keswick School was excellent under Mr Kitching. The choir, I remember, did the *Rio Grande* at one speech day and Vaughan Williams' *Serenade to Music* at another. Every lesson we did some sight-reading using sol-fa on the stave from the Clarendon sight-singing books. We had an annual music festival where not only did we trot out our solo pieces, but we were encouraged to get together in small groups and produce things ourselves. Ron Mustchin taught me violin until Ruth Railton auditioned me for the NYO and decided I was a viola player. She was right. I have had many inspirational teachers but I was never actually taught to teach music. This meant that my pathway as a music educator resulted from having to develop and test materials and methods myself.

Fast forward to 1969. I am in the Bahamas with my husband and baby son. I have been teaching infants for a year. Now the headmaster announces, 'The infants have gone to the other school so you are teaching music to the seniors.' 'But I trained to teach infants.' 'You have an Oxford music degree. You are teaching music to the seniors;' and then the final blow, 'We are buying you a piano.' In the brand new library of the brand new school a single book lies in the middle of the floor. It is not a music book. A truck arrives with a load of unwanted books donated by the Canadian government. The lorry doors open and books spew out. Not boxed, just a heap. In among maths, physics, chemistry, etc. are some music books. I try to think what my mother would do, and assemble in my mind fragments of the Orff and Kodály methods I have seen her use. I pick out some of the songs that don't refer to postmen, rivers or other non-Bahamian things, type out the words, duplicate them on a hand-cranked Banda machine and sew them up into books on my sewing machine. Fortunately the kids like singing, so we sing. Fortunately I can play the guitar, a bit. Fortunately the piano is a long time arriving. At home in England my mother sets to work writing out useful songs for me. She can get about five on an airmail letter. It must have taken her hours. Her beautiful handwriting will come in useful again later.

We buy some steel drums, but before we have time to learn to play them properly we need to play in a concert. I mark the notes of the G chord red and the D chord blue. The children colour the palms of my hands red and blue. We perform our two-chord song perfectly, although my multicoloured conducting style is rather unorthodox. After that I write my first songs, for *The King's New Clothes*. I teach them to all the classes and the actors, from the top class, tour the classrooms doing their thing. I forget how we coped with the nudity. I think we must have imagined it.

'San Salvador teachers' college needs lecturers.' That advertisement changed our lives. They needed married couples, and they needed someone for history (my husband) and someone for music. Well, I'd done it for a year. Why not teach it to teachers? The Bahamian government had decided to set up a teacher training college on San Salvador, in the buildings left behind by the United States when they moved their satellite tracking to Houston. It was an idyllic situation. I started teaching in the students' social club, overlooking the sea, later moving to a handy garage. I had groups of students doing music as a main subject, and everybody taught music when they went out on teaching practice. There was no syllabus, and no guidelines. I possessed, by then, about six books of songs. So the people doing music as a main subject learnt to read and write music, and compose a bit, using what I remembered of Orff and Kodály methods. Everybody made lots of shakers with rice in tins, and sang lots of songs, still provided by my mother, or gradually written by me. I was finally using the skills Bernard Rose had helped me with during my time at Oxford. This time I was able to provide the students with notation, written with a stylus and duplicated on the Gestetner. We had to buy our own paper, so mine was pink to stop my colleagues stealing it.

About a dozen people played the guitar, and I persuaded them to lend their instruments one day a week, so that everybody could have a go. Last year I went back to the Bahamas and met quite a few of my former students, who are now headmistresses, Members of Parliament, lawyers and other dignitaries. They sang me some of the songs I had written for them.

In 1973, when the Bahamas became independent, we were on our way home. My mother had sent an application in my name to James Graham College and the principal, Miss Harland, had invited me to interview because she liked my mother's handwriting. I never found out what information my mother had given about me, or whether any of it was true. Miss Harland asked me to come for one term while she made up her mind. So it was about time I found out how to teach music — and quickly. Jim Wild, who was teaching at Bretton Hall at the time, was a friend of my father's, and was running a DES (Department of Education and Science, as it then was) course for music teachers. It was a great course and I learnt a lot, particularly from Kate Baxter and Michael Stocks. Jim also got me involved with the *Sing for Pleasure* movement, which gave me much useful material, and the opportunity to write more myself. At this time I went to an exhibition of music for schools, and asked one of the reps what he was offering for infants. He said, 'You just take the secondary stuff and adapt it.' So there did seem to be a gap that needed filling.

Once you've written your own stuff it is very difficult to use other people's. By the time you have transposed it and changed the words, it's easier to start from scratch. When I started to do evening classes for teachers, I wrote songs so that they could introduce their children to musical concepts—rhythm patterns, loud and quiet, high and low, etc. That was the beginning of my little books which, thanks to Ray Lovely, and now Carole Lindsay-Douglas, are still on sale. When James Graham College became part of Leeds Polytechnic in 1976 I was asked to teach the graduates who were training for special needs teaching. So I arranged to do some teaching with my husband, who had a special needs class. The head of creative arts said, 'That's okay as long as it doesn't interfere with your work.' When students asked me whether an idea would work for them, at least I could say, 'Well it worked for me yesterday', and where something really dreadful had gone wrong I was able to tell them how to avoid it. Good teaching is an art form and few people get the opportunity to watch it. Taking a group of students to watch a teacher and class who are really comfortable and focused and working hard is a great delight.

The local special needs teachers set up the Yorkshire and Humberside Association for Music in Special Education (YHAMSE). Mavis West and her friends taught me a huge amount—in particular how to break down your teaching into smaller and smaller steps, and how much music can contribute to the overall development of children. Teaching teachers who are themselves starting is fascinating because they can sometimes explain to you the difficulty that they are having. Then you realize that children are having the same difficulty, but don't know how to explain it. I think my love of teaching adults springs from my father's activities with the Women's Institute.

At about this time, Cliff Matthews, music adviser in Wakefield, asked me to write a cantata for the annual music festival. I ended up writing 10 in a row, and learnt a huge amount from watching the teachers teach the children to sing and play them. They also let me take groups of students along each year, which gave them valuable experience. It was exciting to see people working with my music. It's all very well writing it, but putting it over to the children is where the real graft begins, and I am full of admiration for the people who do that. I went on to write all sorts of cantatas on all sorts of subjects for all sorts of people, and I'm still doing this in retirement.

So, what have I learnt?

Well, first of all, my mother was right. Kodály (1929) said:

> If the child is not filled at least once by the life-giving stream of good music during the most susceptible period—between his sixth and sixteenth years—it will hardly be of any use to him later on. Often a single experience will open the young soul to music for a whole lifetime. This experience cannot be left to chance; it is the duty of the school to provide it.

I have met an awful lot of teachers who, when they were at school, were advised to mime while the others were singing. That is not something they are going to forget.

Secondly, in any session you will always learn more things than you teach. The problem is not to beat yourself up about mistakes you have made. Put your special needs hat on and try and work out how you could have made things more simple or accessible. Bribery is always a good idea, whether it is a sticker or a turn to hold a precious toy (chocolate works particularly well with groups of teachers).

Thirdly, steal ideas from everywhere. If you see something done well, you can learn from it. If you see something done badly, you can learn even more from it (and feel smug, too, if you like). In particular, look for ideas that will keep the children focused, high enough to do what you want, but not over the top. Eavesdrop on PE and drama classes. They have the same problem. Keep an eye on the TV. There is no way that we are going to be able to recreate the multitude of noisy and colourful resources available on TV, but you could, for example, buy an unusual toy and write a song about it, or better still, get the children to write a song about it.

Reference

Kodály, Z (1929) Gyermekkarok (Children's Choruses) *Zenei szemle*, xiii/2, pp.1–9. English translation in F. Bonis (ed.) (1974) *The Selected Writings of Zoltán Kodály*. London: Boosey & Hawkes.

A path to self-expression

Jonathan Kirby

I hated music at secondary school. Our first lesson consisted memorably of an enforced audition for the school choir. Beginning with Adams and ending with Woolley, we each had to sing the national anthem solo. The fortunate were stopped after a couple of lines. The less lucky had to persevere into the second verse. The most fortunate of all turned out to be me, however, because inexplicably the teacher jumped from Jones to Lelong, missing Kirby altogether. My father was a clergyman, and I think that was one of the moments in my life when I dabbled with the thought that I might have some special hotline to God.

Similar accidents of fate continued to characterize my musical progress. If there's a theme to my personal musical pathway, it's one of serendipity. Music in school didn't get much better, even with a different teacher who did at least get us to listen to *Rhapsody in Blue*. That was when I learned that music could actually be fun. I also remember being totally awestruck when he invited John Storey, one of my fellow pupils, to play the piano for us in one lesson. We were amazed and delighted with what he played. Playing the piano could be cool. John got much further with the piano than I did. When I was 13, I started lessons. It was too late, and my teacher seemed to hate me even more than I hated her. I didn't even persist to Grade 1. I did opt for Music O-level, for reasons I can't recall. As a 'non-musician', it was dull, seeming to consist of dry academic exercises which I didn't really get on with. I had to drop out, because in October of that O-level year I was knocked off my bicycle and was out for six weeks. That was that. Formal music education had really not been my thing.

Outside school, things were a bit different, though happy accidents were still the theme. One evening, a friend of my parents noticed me tapping along to some music and suggested that I would make a good drummer. Would I like him to teach me? Surprised, and too polite to refuse, I accepted. He brought a snare drum to our house, spent a short time showing me single and double strokes and left me to it. Next week, he returned with a bass drum, hi-hat and another cursory lesson. A couple of weeks later two toms and a couple of cymbals also arrived. He demonstrated at length what was possible and it was only then that it occurred to me that he simply needed somewhere to practise. My parents' Victorian house was much more suitable than his inner-city flat. Nonetheless, I remain forever grateful to Nev Cheetham, because I would never have got started without him.

My sixth-form friends wanted to form a band but there were no drummers. I bought a second-hand Sonor drum kit with the damages I had been paid by the car driver who had knocked me out of school the year before, and my music career had begun. In that band we played mostly covers—Status Quo, Rolling Stones, that sort of thing. I played in another covers band in my first year at Portsmouth Polytechnic as well. In all honesty, I was playing along rather than driving things. I was playing the drums, but I wasn't a drummer. I had been more true to myself in the prog rock trio I was involved with between school and polytechnic, playing along to Emerson Lake and Palmer on the sofa. That was how I learned—playing along to records. I had tried formal drum lessons, but four weeks of playing patterns from a stave on a drum pad were as much as I could endure. I wanted to have fun.

Over the next three years of my French degree course I didn't play very much, though I did guest a few times with a trad jazz band. When I subsequently went to the University of Reading, I found a note in the Students' Union saying 'Drummer wanted. Single imminent'. I signed up, more interested in being on a record than anything else. The horribly-named Bullseye Band did release their single *Why don't you let me know?* which went nowhere, but I made my mark on that record and have been a drummer ever since.

My MA in Left-Wing Thought in 20th-century France more or less guaranteed my unemployability. I got a PGCE and then taught French for four years in a Berkshire comprehensive. I'd taken the job because it enabled me to keep playing with my current band: Spot the Dog were played once by John Peel, so we were very nearly famous. Teaching was great, in theory. In practice, I was dismayed at the lack of enthusiasm for French in school and after four years I had had enough. If you'd told me then that I would be back in schools regularly 14 years later, I simply wouldn't have believed you.

I went full-time into the independent music business. With my brother Tim on bass and vocals and me on drum kit, Diatribe was a duo that got some attention including record releases and the dizzy heights of a session for John Peel—who really was as great a bloke as everyone says. If I had known what taiko was back in those days, the mid 1980s, I would have loved it. It's tempting to say that I was more or less playing taiko on a drum kit in those Diatribe days. A press review describing me as 'one drummer creating a cathedral of sound' was one of my favourites. Unfortunately, Diatribe didn't last very long and I got myself back into employment, this time with Hewlett Packard. I began playing drums for PressGang, a folk-rock group led by Damian Clarke, whose 'single imminent' poster had first hooked me in Reading. PressGang was great fun. I liked Damian's approach of taking traditional music and re-inventing it to make it real for him, real for us. This was a theme I would return to later.

My brother Tim joined another band but it didn't last long because the drummer, Neil Mackie, went to Japan. There, a stranger approached him and told him he would be a taiko drummer. Neil duly trained with him for two years and on his return to the UK, he, Tim and I got together and played some taiko. I was instantly hooked, but I was on the point of moving to California with my family for a new job with Hewlett Packard. Neil said there was a group near where I was going, and gave me a phone number.

For those still unacquainted with it, taiko is highly-choreographed team drumming played on a range of different-sized drums. Its roots are in Japan, but taiko drumming of the kind now seen all round the world was created in the 1950s by a jazz drummer called Daihachi Oguchi, whose personal hero was Art Blakey. Once I arrived in California I called the number Neil had given me. I went for interview and was accepted on an audition process that started just 10 days later, and would last 11 months. As the training progressed, I realized I had signed up for one of the leading professional taiko groups in the USA. I had had no idea that San Jose Taiko was so prestigious a group, or I wouldn't have dared make that initial phone call. They were the only group in the USA to provide in-depth training that included the history and culture as well as the technicalities and physicalities of taiko. The more I learned with them, and the more I played taiko, the less I wanted to do anything else. I loved taiko and I loved the way that San Jose Taiko went about it, creating their own, original taiko based on an understanding of the traditions, but allowing their music to be influenced by their own Californian culture.

It was tempting to stay in California for taiko alone but, along with my wife and three young children, I really missed England, our families and friends. I was convinced that there ought to be more taiko in England. Education and performance combined with missionary zeal and all wrapped up in drumming—what could be better? It made sense of my drumming career, my business experience with Hewlett Packard and the teaching experience I had had before that. Nonetheless, it was a huge risk. For two years we had to scrape a living from a minimal income and savings that rapidly dwindled to nothing. Money doesn't buy happiness, however, and I have never regretted leaving the Hewlett Packard job behind.

I wasn't alone in taking taiko into schools in the late 1990s. A handful of others had returned from Japan, but they were often using taiko to recreate the cultural experience they had had there. As far as I was concerned, taiko was fun and exciting and it was a vehicle for much broader learning. Two years of taiko training didn't make me a great taiko player, still less did it make me a great taiko teacher, but my experiences at San Jose convinced me that I could develop my own way of working.

My own way proved long and hard, with trial and error and lots of adventure. I took workshops when and where I could. I organized visits and exchanges with other groups from Japan and the USA. I watched and learned, I experimented and welcomed feedback. My own groups provided the test-beds for teaching ideas. They also enabled me to develop a suite of original repertoire over the years. It had been clear to me from the beginning that an approach based on culture would not be the best. For one thing, I'm not Japanese. For another, Japanese methods aren't appropriate in this country. I had my first falling-out with a Japanese father in the primary school where I launched my first school group. He wanted to help but was appalled at the idea of the children performing in assembly at the end of term. 'They will not be good enough to perform for at least two years' he insisted. This Japanese approach to 'total quality control' was very different from the culture of 'showing and telling' that we enjoy here. Other people confuse form with content, insisting on Japanese-style discipline and ritual as if that is what taiko is all about. To play taiko, you don't have to pretend to be Japanese and you certainly don't have to play Japanese repertoire. To be authentic, you have to make it your own, as Damian Clarke had shown me in PressGang and as PJ Hirabayashi had shown me at San Jose Taiko. This is part of the joy of taiko—it's a really great way of being yourself.

This approach certainly stood me in good stead with visiting groups. We have been honoured with visits from San Jose Taiko, Kodo and, in 2004, Daihachi Oguchi himself, the man who started it all. In 2005, my juniors were invited by the Nippon Taiko Foundation to perform in Tokyo, alongside the junior taiko champions of Japan. I don't actively seek approval from all these people, I'm happy to do my own thing in a principled and carefully considered way. Nonetheless, it was great to get this kind of validation for my approach. I've now been a taiko professional for nearly 14 years. It's the longest I've done anything, apart from being a husband and father. It's been an exciting adventure and promises to continue to be so. As with any true adventure it's unpredictable, perhaps less now than at the outset, but surprises do keep happening. It's certainly not a career I had planned when at school or at university. Having said that, I do remember walking home from school one afternoon with Gary Glitter's *Rock and Roll Part 2* going through my head. It sounded like nothing I'd ever heard before and was very drum-oriented. I thought, 'Wouldn't it be great to invent a new form of drum-based music like that?' This was more an envious thought than an intention, but maybe there was something there that guided me through the string of happy accidents and led me to where I am now.

So why do we need music education?

Dominique Laviolette

The truth is, I did not get involved in music through the belief that it might be useful as a career. I immersed myself in music out of sheer passion and interest. I have long held a belief that the most important thing children can learn from education is how to think effectively; to access the power of their brains. I became enthralled by music at the age of seven because it made me think—of things to play, how to play them, how to change them, how to listen, how to copy and so forth. Music was something of a gym for my brain, a real workout that I enjoyed and so kept coming back. I would love to suggest complex reasons for first getting involved in music but it was just that simple—I absolutely loved playing the keyboard and creating new things.

Many musicians talk of being surrounded by music throughout their youth, having parents who played instruments, or performing in shows and events from a young age. For me, however, apart from my father occasionally tinkering with a beat-up acoustic guitar and my sister being an enthusiastic electronic organ player, there was no real sense of musicality flowing through our household. I was taken by my father to keyboard lessons at the same place that my sister learned to play the organ, but I soon quit because I didn't want to learn how to read music. I thought, 'I've been having fun playing without these symbols, so why should I now have to learn using these boring instructions, when I can just listen and copy?' For a while, this worked and I was able to look at the tutor's hands and listen to what he was playing and then play the piece as if I had learnt from the dots on the page. However, this could only go on for so long and so I quit lessons and continued playing as I had before. I wanted to enjoy music on *my* terms. I think that most parents would have interfered at that point and attempted to guide their child to persevere with the dots. Crucially, and rather admirably, my father did nothing. Instead he just allowed his young son to discover and do as he pleased.

After quitting piano lessons, I was less focused on music. I spent my time playing football and taking this very seriously. I suppose that because all my friends were involved in football—playing for teams, training twice a week, playing for the school and at every spare moment during the summer breaks—there was an attraction there for me. None of my friends was in the slightest bit interested in music and so it followed that I lost interest too; I was not surrounded by a 'music community' at the time.

I still enjoyed playing the keyboard during my spare time at home and I also chose music as one of my options for Key Stage 4. For a short while after my parents purchased our first home computer, I became addicted to a music program called

Evolution—almost identical to Cubase. I would sit for hours and compose songs using the QWERTY keyboard. This was my first foray into composition. I had little knowledge of what I was actually doing but I had an understanding of musicality, using chords and adding tones with fairly complex layered rhythms. I could not believe there existed software that gave me an unlimited number of tracks, with countless sounds from pianos to strings, and the ability to instantly edit and make decisions. The process of working alone without having to explain my musical decisions to other musicians or teachers was an important phase of my music education.

Then, when I was fifteen, my father bought me a keyboard workstation with a sixteen-track sequencer. So began a tide of composition that has lasted to this day. I still have the floppy disks of the compositions I produced on this keyboard over a five-year period. I was now surrounded by music with the subject now forming a large chunk of my Key Stage 4 study and my new instrument to come home to every day.

I showed the songs to my music and drama teachers and was encouraged by their approval. As a result, I moved on to Music Technology at A-level where I met a very influential music teacher. Upon meeting him at the open evening, he asked me, 'What instrument do you play?' I replied that I didn't play an instrument, 'Just the keyboard', to which he responded, 'But . . . that is an instrument. Of course it is. You play the keyboard.' My lack of formal tuition had led me to believe that I could not possibly be classified as a performer who played an instrument—I just dabbled within my own rules, I thought. However, this teacher encouraged me to take my skills seriously and I began to explore further the option of being both a composer and serious performer. I began to see the piano not only as a compositional tool but also as an instrument to express myself. My compositions began to inform my skills as a pianist and vice versa.

Again, my community dictated my actions. I was now surrounded by musicians—including the teacher—who lived and breathed music, and the prospect of professional football began to fade. There were pianists far more advanced than I thought 'normal' for the age we were at, singers, brass players, and many more. Our lessons involved the teacher pacing up and down, talking about the reasons why the Beatles had become so revered and why Bach was so important for western classical music, always waving his hands as if he had too much information in his mind to physically get out of his mouth. I had never been in such a stimulating environment. The presence of so many enthusiastic musicians made me want to do interesting and innovative things with my own music. Had I not been in such an environment then I doubt that I would have thought of a career in music as an achievable goal. My previous idea of having a career in music conjured up thoughts of pop stars and celebrities; I'd never heard of musicians making a living any other way than through the pop charts. Yet I now began to think of becoming a musician first and foremost, then deciding where to go once I was happy with my abilities.

I left college to pursue a degree in Music Technology, where I was surrounded by technology 'geeks', for some of whom music was just a product they worked with. There was never a piano in any of the teaching rooms, just stacks of expensive audio recording equipment. At first I believed that gaining a knowledge of recording could help me to be self-sufficient as a musician and producer. However, I soon quit, realizing that I was no longer composing and playing music and that being an audio engineer took my focus away from the music itself. Nevertheless, I used the knowledge gained to set up a small home studio and embarked upon another phase of composition. Without doubt those next years were important in shaping my musical persona today. I spent all my time at home during the day composing and recording my songs and listening critically to the results.

After listening to little but my own music for six years, I realized that I needed specialist help to move on further. I was afraid of having a tutor who would insist that I learn to read notation and become one of those pupils who performs piece after piece mechanically, with little passion. I opted for a jazz tutor in the belief that this style of music would give me the ability to toy with harmony and chords as I so wanted. Almost 15 years after abandoning tuition, I finally found a tutor who said I didn't have to read music if I didn't want to and who could help me with my piano skills. His words were, 'You can learn whatever you want to learn, and I'll help you with that.' Having a teacher fuelled my desire to become better and expand my musical knowledge and from here things sky-rocketed and took me to where I am now—about to begin my PGCE and, I hope, become a music teacher. Yet it is also a prerequisite of being a music educator that I have to learn about the theoretical knowledge and information that I earlier turned away from in favour of playing.

Unlike most of my musical peers, I never appeared on stage until my late twenties; I never took part in music shows or events; I was never part of any band or ensemble. It wasn't until I reached 16 that I really took an interest in music and thereafter things began to snowball. There was no right or wrong path that I knew of. The result is that I hold an informal approach to learning music in high regard. I have become a musician who promotes what I would call the 'natural' process of music-making—discovery, listening and learning by ear, without any hard and fast rules of how any single thing should be done. On the one hand, I have a tendency to be intimidated by the rules and theory of western classical music. I often look at a music score and wilt at the thought of having to decode the notes on the page in any time-scale quicker than a day. With regard to notation and music terminology, my musical past is a disadvantage. On the other hand, I am grateful that I can sit at a piano and play something musical in any circumstance.

I think that my early beginnings have given me an insight into the essentially human nature of music-making: we are all 'natural musicians' and we will always create music. In my formative years, no-one told me how music should be played or created. Instead, I listened to other musicians and made up my own mind. Sometimes I think that formal lessons can be artificial and contrived.

For me, the biggest impact has been the power of music itself. I could maybe best describe music as a catalyst for success in everything I do, simply because it encourages me to think and explore my own mind. The experience of spending years as a musician playing, experimenting, failing and so on, has informed my judgement on life in general. I know that things can take time, through having taken the time to learn to be a musician. I know that failures, large or small, are inevitable and cannot be predicted—having failed many times at many things while learning as a musician.

Most importantly, I have learned of the value of having a focus in my life, and how valuable it can be for others to have a focus that encompasses and challenges them.

I can look back and realize that my favourite teachers were those who made me aspire to greater things. Their enthusiasm was incredibly infectious. I wanted to know what it was that made their minds spark and I sought to acquire that same enthusiasm through attaining knowledge, guided by them. That was my learning. This pathway—of inspiring me to think—is what made me want to continue with music and to pass on that inspiration through teaching.

I can't imagine a life without music!

Julian Lloyd Webber

I cannot remember a time without music. My mother specialized in teaching young children the piano and, in my earliest years, my father was still composing. I grew up surrounded by music, hearing all kinds of music all the time. My mother's pupils would come to our flat and my father would either be composing every morning at the piano or be practising the organ on a special piano he had fitted with pedals in his study. In later years, John Lill, who had joined the household as a lodger, would practise the piano furiously all day long and my brother Andrew would be composing on yet another piano. It was a cacophony of sound and it was a wonder that we were not all thrown out of the top-floor flat in the Victorian London mansion block that housed the Lloyd Webber 'menagerie'.

I first saw a cello when I was four. I was taken to one of the Ernest Read orchestral concerts at the Royal Festival Hall and I remember being captivated by the *look* of the cello being played and asking if I could try one. When a tenth-sized instrument arrived at the flat I was pretty disappointed that it wasn't as big as the magnificent specimens I had seen at the Festival Hall that day. But I enjoyed playing it and I was soon spending a lot of time with my new toy.

By the time I was nine I was going to the Royal College of Music's Junior Department every Saturday morning and an important turning point arrived when, aged 11, I had a new teacher called Rhuna Martin. Memory tells me that Rhuna was an attractive young lady from South Africa—not long out of music college herself—and it was Rhuna who really encouraged my interest in the cello. For instead of emphasizing technique, she talked about the music itself. More importantly—and way beyond her call of duty—she began taking me to hear really good cellists in concert. (Strangely the first one I heard was the great Pierre Fournier, with whom I came to study more than 20 years later.)

Rhuna was prepared to let me loose on more advanced pieces just because I liked them. I realize now that this was crucial, as it was only when I decided *myself* that I wanted to play a piece of music that I really started practising it properly. She encouraged me to follow my own path and I soon became fixated—almost to the point of obsession—on the cello repertoire. While other little boys were collecting cigarette cards I was collecting obscure cello concertos. I would look up the listings in *Radio Times* and tape any performances of solo cello music I could find. I still have those reel to reel tapes today and I can tell you there are some gems amongst them.

Later, when I was 13, I had another new teacher, Douglas Cameron, who had a tremendous knowledge of the cello and its repertoire. His style of teaching—often supported by copious cigarettes and tumblers full of whisky—would definitely be outlawed today but he, too, concentrated on music rather than technique and I learned a huge amount from him. Jacqueline du Pré used to call William Pleeth her 'cello daddy' and Cameron was certainly mine. Above all, he loved the instrument and I can see now that the teachers who brought the best out of me were the ones who encouraged me in my love of music rather than 'banging on' about how I should be holding the bow. Of course, you need technique to be able to play more intricate pieces but if you are filled with enthusiasm for the music then that will lead you to find your own solutions for technical problems.

Another life-changing event occurred for me when I was 13: the great Russian cellist Rostropovich came to London and gave a cycle of nine concerts in which he covered almost all of the existing cello repertoire—though, even then, I was mildly miffed to note that he didn't play the Delius, Walton or—perhaps more surprisingly—Khachaturian cello concertos. But I loved his approach to the cello. In his programme note for the series he described the instrument as 'a hero for our times'. I also admired his determination to expand the cello repertoire and it was marvellous to hear all these new works that he inspired for the cello by composers like Prokofiev, Shostakovich and Britten—what a legacy!

I admit that I always wanted to be a soloist—because that was how I heard the cello as an instrument. Yet, even though—or maybe even because—I grew up in a musical environment, I was constantly told that it was impossible to be a solo cellist. In the early 1960s you could count the number of cellists who made a living as a soloist on one—or at a stretch, two—hands. But, of course, the more I was told it was an impossible dream the more determined I became to do it.

It is vital to take every possible opportunity to play in public when you are starting out. In my last years at the Royal College I did every possible audition I could. But my biggest break came through the college itself. In May 1971 I played Prokofiev's monumental *Sinfonia Concertante* at its President's Concert. The College orchestra was conducted by Vernon Handley and the second half consisted of a work by the College President, Sir Arthur Bliss. Sir Arthur was in attendance and, the next day, he sent me a score (c/o the College) of his own cello concerto, which had just been premiered by Rostropovich himself at the Aldeburgh Festival. Although he hadn't actually asked me to perform it, I determined to learn it. I arranged to go to his house with a pianist from college and play it to him. I had never been so nervous in my entire life—but it must have gone OK because, soon after, I discovered that he had personally suggested I should give the first London performance of the concerto in September 1972. This was not only an extraordinary honour for me but also a fantastic opportunity, having left College just two months before.

Although I had been awarded a scholarship to study with Pierre Fournier—who was based in Geneva—I had already made a decision to base myself in this country. I knew it was vital to build up a career early on, and I took on any job that would give me the experience of playing in public because only through playing to an audience can you learn how to communicate music.

Looking back, I am hugely aware of the fundamental role that my musical family life played in my own development. Had I not been born into such a background I have no idea whether I would have become a musician or not. What *is* certain is that musical education must begin young in order for anyone to have a chance of becoming a professional musician. And, in the absence of music being part of the home, then access to music has to come from schools, which is why I believe so passionately that music should be a birthright available to *all* children — not just the privileged few whose parents can afford to buy instruments and pay for music tuition.

This core belief is what attracted me so much to *In Harmony*, the Government-backed programme which I have chaired since its beginning three years ago. I already had a long-standing interest in music education and, in 2003, James Galway, Evelyn Glennie and I had formed the Music Education Consortium to lobby on behalf of better provision for music in schools. The government's response was the Music Manifesto, launched in 2004. At first I could not support it because, although the intentions were good, it was not backed up by any financial commitment. However, after the government announced its unprecedented £332 million support for music education in 2007 I was very happy to do so.

A small part — in percentage terms — of that new development was *In Harmony*, the programme inspired by Venezuela's legendary *El Sistema* movement, which uses music as a catalyst to bring communities together. In 2007 I saw the Simón Bolívar Youth Orchestra's sensational performance at the Proms and, as a result of an interview I gave afterwards to *The Observer,* I was invited by the government to set up a similar project in this country. The results from the three existing projects have been extraordinary and have exceeded all expectations. No one working in music education in this country should see *In Harmony* as anything but a massively helpful adjunct to existing organizations. For instance, good players that come through the *In Harmony* programme need not be channelled into separate *In Harmony* orchestras, but could feed into existing ones. The difference is that these players would be coming from social groups who would otherwise have never had that opportunity.

In November 2009 I visited Venezuela at the invitation of *El Sistema*'s founder, José Antonio Abreu, who wanted me to observe it at first hand. It was the first time that I had seen *El Sistema* in action and, in all honesty, there had been so much excitement about it in the musical world that I was quite prepared to be disappointed. Instead I returned convinced that the project's huge potential for both social and musical regeneration is the future for music education in the 21st century.

In some ways, access to every kind of music has never been easier. The internet is a fantastic resource where you can see so many different performances and listen to every conceivable piece of music. Yet young players often seem to lack even the most basic curiosity about their instrument's repertoire and seem content to coast by on what they are given to play by their teachers. My best advice for anyone starting now on their musical journey is to develop that curiosity, to explore all the music that is now so freely available. That is the way to discover your road as yet untravelled — your own personal musical pathway.

The distinctiveness principle

Bill C. Martin

Beginnings

In many ways ours was a conventional south-east London working-class family. My father worked long night shifts transforming hot metal into printers' type for *The Times*; we lived in a council house; we had no money for luxuries and were one of the last families locally to get a car or TV. And we certainly couldn't afford to spend money on leisure activities at the weekends. So, and this is where my family was quite unconventional, at weekends, my parents, family and friends would often descend on us and the evenings would soon develop into a party, where people of all generations would chat and take turns to sing, play the piano, guitar or accordion.

None of my family ever had formal music lessons. They worked their music out by ear and memory, often during these weekend sessions. This was usually accompanied by impassioned discussions about the melody or the best chord to use at a certain point in a song, continuing until a consensus had been reached. Though my father and grandfather could play only in the keys of D and G, they played with such soul and passion that, even as a four-year-old in 1959, I was often moved to tears by it. I remember lying in bed and listening to the wonderful music soaring up from downstairs. Their repertoire was mainly the popular songs and standards they had grown up, with but you knew it was 'their' music as soon as they played.

Before my fifth birthday my father and grandfather began teaching me a few of their songs, *What'll I Do* being one of the first, in a simplified arrangement with chords in the left hand and the tune in the right. I was so excited to be able to make my performance debut at a family gathering at the age of five. The applause and encouragement I received made me hunger for more and I loved the sessions where someone would painstakingly teach me something new, in a 'listen, watch and copy' kind of approach. It worked brilliantly and, looking back on it, was some of the most patient, insightful, inspiring and effective teaching I've ever experienced.

My parents somehow managed to find some money for 'proper' piano lessons with a local teacher. I hated it! He lacked the patience of my 'untutored' family members and shouted at me a lot. So I stopped having lessons with him. In other circumstances I would surely have been turned off music altogether, but my father and grandfather offered to do more, by way of compensation.

I learned more of their popular song repertoire, which we played mostly in a stride piano style. My grandfather, with a left-hand stretch of a twelfth, seemed to use every one of the 88 keys and just made it sing. Around the age of six, they showed me how to work out all major, minor, 7th, diminished and augmented chords. It was one thing to be taught how to play a particular piece of music; it was something else to be given the tools to work music out for myself.

It strikes me that the music education sector could multiply its impact by helping parents understand the value of family music-making at home, perhaps even training them to be able to support it. This shared family activity was the foundation for everything else that has happened in my music and teaching career.

Breadth and depth

At the age of nine I was sent to another, far better, local piano teacher. I was now hungry to learn all kinds of music, regardless of genre. The things I'd already learned about the workings of harmony, melody and the way a piece builds in excitement during a good performance seemed to be common to all music, including the classical repertoire. My teacher worked hard to develop my ability to play from a score and put me through the ABRSM piano syllabus, mostly with merits and distinctions.

By the time I went to Chislehurst and Sidcup Grammar School, music was a central part of my identity. I learned folk guitar, which later sparked a deep love affair with the British, American and European folk traditions, and taught a close school friend, too. I sang in choirs and madrigal groups, played in rock and folk bands and was even allowed to play a piano part with the school orchestra. I composed for the school orchestra and for school plays.

The head of music, Ron Halford, coached me through A-level music, and also taught me church organ. But it was an assistant music teacher, Derek Barnes, whose impact has most profoundly shaped my career. Derek was also a professional arranger, composer and singer. In my final years at school he gave me singing lessons, taught me techniques of arranging and composing and introduced me to contemporary classical music. My singing lessons with Derek followed the vocal method that his own teacher, Derek Hammond-Stroud, had been developing. Singing bass in choirs and as an occasional soloist throughout my school career, my vocal range expanded by a fifth, thanks to Derek's inspired teaching.

At this time I'd heard Ligeti's gorgeous, other-worldly music that had been used for Kubrick's *2001: A Space Odyssey*. That was my first encounter with music that didn't use conventional rhythm, melody and harmony. The opportunity to compose, with Derek's guidance, in a non-tonal style was also very exciting for me.

My musical education until I left school had been a real voyage of discovery. I sometimes feel sorry for young people whose music education is not built on developing performing skills as the pathway to a first-hand understanding of what music is about. Our curriculum in English schools still largely ignores the importance of progressive performing skills, which remain available largely to a privileged minority, and mostly outside curriculum time. No wonder young people have voted with their feet in recent years and not opted for music at KS4. Only by giving young people real music-making skills and tools can they truly realize their own musical ambitions.

Towards a career in music

I gained a teaching diploma with Trinity College London and studied on the BMus (Hons) degree course at Royal Holloway College, London University. I studied composition and was introduced to a wealth of exciting new music and ideas. Though mine was an academic degree, much of my university life was spent in practical music-making: composing for theatre, performing with the experimental music ensemble, singing in college operettas and running the folk club.

Though piano remained my first instrument, I never felt I had much to contribute as a conventional pianist. In any case my composing, arranging and growing interest in both experimental and early music occupied my creative processes completely. I had no career path in mind, other than wanting to earn my living through music and teaching. If I was going to make my mark I had to find something distinctive which would enable me to get professional work because of that distinctiveness.

While at Royal Holloway I formed the house band to run the college folk club. The line-up eventually settled as a quintet, and the band Pyewackett was born. Band members sang and played keyboards, guitar, bass guitar, whistles, recorders, clarinet, saxophones, hammered dulcimer, bassoon, sordune (a Renaissance-era double reed instrument), violin, viola and occasionally drums. This unconventional line-up came about simply because these were the instruments a group of music students with catholic musical tastes happened to play. For a budding arranger this was a real windfall; the opportunity to experiment with and learn about such rich timbres and how best to manipulate them taught me much in a very short time.

Pyewackett evolved after my graduation in 1977, with a repertoire ranging from troubadour songs and Playford dance tune arrangements to early jazz, folk songs, minimalism and even some pop music. The closest we came to categorizing it was 'pop music from the last five centuries'. It led to extensive European tours, headlining at European folk festivals, four albums, a residency on BBC Radio 4's *The Song Tree* and a growing demand for me to work as a session musician. I was mostly being booked because I had created a sound that was fairly unique. My distinctiveness strategy was working.

A chance decision after one enormously enjoyable session as arranger and keyboard player, led me to take the 'points'—a share of the record sales if we ever sold any—instead of a session fee. Thankfully, 'Star Trekkin' sold almost 500,000 copies in the UK and several million around the world, compensating me for more meaningful musical projects which had earned very little.

Music Educator

Since my first learning experiences with family members, I knew that teaching would always be part of my career. I taught A-level music in one south-east London school and worked as a piano and guitar teacher in several others.

My interest and expertise in electronic instruments and recording technology had grown. At the same time, the National Curriculum had been born and teachers needed help in getting to grips with recording equipment and designing schemes of work for new genres and instruments. These were exactly my skills and I wrote to several musical instrument manufacturers to see if they would support me in providing music technology workshops for secondary music teachers.

The only one which seemed to have a genuine and long-term vision for music education was Yamaha and they asked me to run some sessions for teachers attending a music trade fair in London. This led to extensive freelance work touring more workshops for secondary class teachers, provided free by Yamaha.

I probably learned more about teaching during this time than I'd ever done before, probably because I built in time for reflection. I became aware of so many shortcomings in my thinking and in how I taught that I completely revised my approach to one which engaged not only with curriculum content but with identifying and overcoming some of the psychological and social barriers to learning, in both children and adults.

Courses and publications

Having written course outlines for my composing activities and published a book of progressive classroom ensemble arrangements with Chester Music, I was asked by several schools and colleges to help them write courses and course modules covering composing and keyboard playing. I developed this strand further when, in the early 1990s, a business partner and I set up Coda, a music centre near Christchurch, Dorset. Initially we ran workshops for children; weekly group lessons in keyboard, guitar, singing and violin; seminars for composers on ways to work in education; and training for teachers and lecturers in music technology.

I left Coda in 1996 to join Yamaha and develop new keyboard and guitar courses for their UK music schools. Over a 12-year period we produced courses which had real breadth and depth and saw an explosion of interest in keyboard and guitar playing. My own broad experiences had provided me with more musical choices than most other musicians I know. Such breadth became a central tenet of our courses. My goal was to give young people real musical choices through a broad, mostly teacher-led, core curriculum, which had to provide demonstrable skills and progression, derived from content which balanced ears and eyes, emotion and intellect. In this way, at whatever point learners decided to stop their lessons, they would have become independent, thinking musicians with a good chance of tackling almost any musical situation.

My experiences so far have given me a strong drive to be distinctive and achieve the best at what I do, and to help others do the same. I've deliberately evolved this into a personal 'brand' which is now recognized across the music and music education sectors. The work I do now, as Yamaha UK's music education manager, enables me to engage with an extraordinarily wide range of partners, including conservatoire principals and professors, teachers, gifted and talented young musicians, Yamaha international artists, MPs, music services, a broad range of organizations, young musicians and their families. Central to all of this is the importance of listening and communicating effectively. Fortunately it is what good musicians do best.

More information about the strategies referred to above for overcoming psychological and social barriers to learning can be found on the Musical Pathways section of the NAME website (www.name.org/publications).

Connecting mainstream and SEN— bridging the gap musically

Paul McDowell

Like many children brought up in the eighties in the UK, I grew up listening to the radio and my parents' records. My grandfather would often sing at the dinner table, my father played piano regularly in the evenings, and my mother frequently performed with a local amateur dramatics society. Growing up in Liverpool, I started writing my own songs from around seven or eight years old and my parents encouraged me to learn the piano and the cello. I achieved Grade 6 piano and Grade 5 theory before focusing my efforts on the guitar at thirteen, when I started to write songs more prolifically, passing Grade 4 classical guitar before focusing on more popular styles of music. I also sang in the choir, took lead parts in school musicals and plays, and was a cellist in the school orchestra. I formed a band with some school friends and we would practise regularly after school, playing songs that I had written. Growing up near the beach, I would often play the guitar and sing around campfires for fun. My song writing has always been greatly influenced by nature, words, feelings, and life experiences; and I have always found that music provides a perfect portal for poetical self-expression.

However, my parents were concerned that the direction the music industry was taking would make it more difficult to support myself and a family financially in the future if I was to take on a career in music. Taking their advice, I went down the scientific route in school and university, continuing to play and write music in my spare time. After finishing my BSc degree I moved to London to try to make it as a musician, but I struggled to pay rent, working in a gig venue at night and writing songs during the daytime. After six months, a university friend asked me to attend a job interview at a prestigious city firm, where I was employed as a graduate surveyor, which corresponded with my BSc degree. However, I continued to write songs in every spare minute and could not get away from my fixation with and passion for music.

After six months working in the city I returned to the University of Reading to study for a Masters in Planning and Development alongside a Diploma in Computer Music Production at the local Arts College, my first step into musical academia at the tender age of 22. Music technology expanded my musical horizons and enabled me to record the songs that I had been writing over the years.

Upon completion of my masters, I moved back to Liverpool and spent the next seven years of my life devoted to making music. Along the way I played many gigs as well as working as a fundraiser for charities, a bar man, a gig organizer and promoter, and a DJ. In the lulls I claimed jobseekers allowance. Fortunately I was eligible for the Government's New Deal for Musicians. This enabled me to study Music Business at the Liverpool Institute of Performing Arts (LIPA), where I was invited to meet, and play some of my music to, Sir Paul McCartney. I was awarded a distinction and the course led me to gain experience in a variety of colleges, helping out in music workshops. At LIPA I also met Steve Powell, a renowned music producer based in the North West, who recorded my first EP. With my guitar, voice and my new EP, I made several tours in the UK and Europe, playing gigs in various cities.

Over the years I have played music with a wide range of musicians, all of whom I feel lucky to have met and learnt from. As well as leading several bands, I find that playing in a variety of supportive roles in different musical groups has helped me to understand many approaches to music. Hours of informal jam sessions with different musicians have taught me many musical skills that I just could not have learnt in individual practice. Besides playing music with them, one of the great things about knowing other musicians is finding out about the music that inspires them. Listening to music has become increasingly important to me and when I am not making music I am more often than not listening to it. The people I have met over the years have introduced me to countless bands and artists who I may not have heard of otherwise.

In 2008, I met Mike Perry in Liverpool, a talented drummer with whom I formed a two piece band. We have spent many hours writing and playing music and experimenting musically together in informal settings in a variety of studios and spaces. His experimental drumming style opened up new avenues musically, also introducing me to a wider range of music to listen to. I have also recently started jamming with a wide range of other musicians, including Felix Hatton, an enthusiastic music man.

In 2009, I moved to Berlin, a city I had grown fond of after playing there on previous tours. At one of my gigs, I met Gordon Raphael, a professional music producer, who invited me to record at his studio. We spent a pleasant afternoon recording some of my solo acoustic songs together. After six months of writing songs, recording and playing gigs there, I returned home to Liverpool. My mother is a physiotherapist in Rowan Park SEN School, and, in fact, the first time I sang and played guitar outside lessons and home — my first gig — was to a group of SEN children that she works with. I was considering becoming a teaching assistant, and my mother put me in touch with Rowan Park, which gave me the opportunity of shadowing the music teacher. Seeing the effect that the music had on the students in comparison with other subjects made me realize how important music is for these children. Soon after that I went to work in a Youth Centre in the inner city. I facilitated musical activities with the children, encouraging them to express themselves musically. This included song writing, group singing and group drumming sessions with a variety of percussion.

It was around this time that I heard of London Metropolitan University's two-year route into music teaching for those without a music degree, but with sufficient knowledge, experience and passion for the art. I decided to apply and, after a rigorous audition process, I was delighted to be accepted on the course.

Before moving to London I contacted many after-school schemes in London, hoping to continue my work in a musical capacity related to my experience in the Youth Centre and the SEN school. I was fortunate enough to be accepted at an after-school scheme at The Bridge Special School, where I continue to organize music activities with secondary SEN pupils. I find it particularly rewarding to make music with these pupils because every day presents new challenges and behaviours, giving them the opportunity to express themselves through singing and playing music. Music seems to connect with them at a very profound level and it provides them with an outlet which other forms of communication may not offer. I always start the sessions with a familiar welcome song, followed by any number of musical activities, including exploration of different instruments and sounds, song writing, and singing and playing interactive songs. Using props, themes, Makaton sign language and other materials helps the children listen, understand and relate to the music, and making music out of silence works wonders.

In September 2010 I commenced my course at London Metropolitan University. Upon finding out about my experience with SEN pupils, the course leader, David Cross, put me in touch with David Jackson, who organizes musical activities in special needs schools using Assistive Music Technology. I spent a few days with him at Meldreth Manor, an independent special school run by Scope. Here I gained experience of how Soundbeam technology can provide children with profound learning difficulties with further opportunities for musical exploration through movement. This taught me the need for a large musical repertoire and helped me to understand that adaptability is also essential, considering the ever changing and unexpected behaviours and musical responses of these amazing children.

I continue to spend increasing time and effort learning more about the academic side of music in order to be able to teach it in mainstream secondary schools, while also composing and writing music when the inspiration arrives. All of my tutors at London Metropolitan University have taught me invaluable lessons, and the school placements, essay writing and large variety of books available have helped me to reflect on how best to approach teaching music. I am about to commence my second (PGCE) year and am excited about what the future holds.

Incidental music

Alice Nicholls

My introduction to music was in part accidental, and it began with *The Old Mole*. I was six years old and trying, without much success, to play the recorder in our school Christmas play. We'd been given a simple tune, only eight bars or so, which the Year 3s were to dance to. It was the recorder group's only opportunity to shine. So imagine my disappointment—not to say humiliation—when I was told I would be playing 'the easy part', which was all of three notes. The following day, I stomped up to my room and refused to come out. After a few hours my mother came and found me, having heard odd squeaky noises coming from behind the door. The odd squeaky noises were my attempts to learn, by heart, the seemingly impossible eight bars of *The Old Mole*. I didn't come down for tea until I'd mastered it.

Roll forward a few years and I had moved on from the descant and had started teaching myself the treble recorder. Our school, at which my mother was a teacher, had just received the go-ahead to provide instrumental lessons to pupils. 'Do you want to try it, just to make up numbers?' my mum had pleaded with me. The choice was violin or cello, and I decided on violin, eventually carrying it on in secondary school and joining a youth orchestra. Music came easily to me, more so than scientific or mathematical subjects. When I began learning the notes—the mechanics of the music—it was like learning a new language, but unlike French or German, which I later struggled with, all the words just seemed to make sense. There was no past or future tense, no grammatical regulations, it was all so simple—B was always this note, D was always this line, etc. Although at that age I had no idea why I found it so easy, it seems fairly obvious in hindsight. There had been music in my household for as long as I can remember. My mother played flute in a concert band and sang in a choir, and every lesson at school was permeated with a song or musical activity where possible. Musical ability was fostered, encouraged, and nurtured—I think my parents knew I would be good at it before I did.

I stuck with music, trying out various new instruments and discovering that I wasn't a bad singer, and was eventually told by my class teacher that if I didn't take music as a GCSE subject then he would personally shoot me in the foot. Ever since then I have used music as a way to prove myself to others—to my peers, my teachers, and as a backlash to my own anxieties. I stopped myself getting bullied in Year 11 by getting up and singing in front of my classmates; I proved every male musician in our school wrong when I took up the bass guitar; and as a result I proved to myself that I had talent. Cue me taking music first to GCSE, then A-level, then to degree level, and now finally to postgraduate study in music therapy.

I moved to Huddersfield to study music at the age of eighteen. Two major events happened during the course of my degree. The first was that I got diagnosed, in my first year, with depression, which paved the way for the next four years to be a constant stream of doctors' appointments, therapy, medication and self-doubt. The second—and the two are by no means unrelated—was my rising interest in this thing I had discovered called 'music therapy'.

Prior to starting my degree course, I volunteered at the Orpheus Centre—a residential home that provides performing arts courses for disabled adults—and have gone back there to volunteer at least once a year since, because of the amazing work they do there. At the time, in the summer of 2006, my older brother was toying with the idea of becoming a special needs teacher, and our mum had heard of this amazing facility (i.e. the Centre), and urged us to volunteer. I was intrigued to see how on earth people with such severe disabilities could be expected to write music, much less get up on stage and perform it. It was a steep learning curve. In truth, the place was probably as good for me as it was for the students I worked with—it was incredibly humbling to see how they each coped with their disabilities (some of which were very severe), how they were able to make jokes about it, write songs about it, get a laugh from it, and the solidarity they had with each other. I remember a particular student who had just got a new wheelchair at the start of the week. She was so fed up with getting sent the wrong foot plates that she decided to write a comedy song about it: it ended up being the funniest story of the week. It was in a way life-affirming to see some of these disabled students, and there are two particular women Rachel and Catherine (not their real names) to whom I owe thanks, because it is their stories and the work we did together that helped to set me on the path to a career in music therapy.

Catherine had been a student at the Centre from about the time I started volunteering there; she had pronounced autism and an incredibly nervous disposition. In the first week I was there I doubt that she said more than two words to me. When I returned to the Centre the following year, we were paired up to work together. I learned that, like me, she was a violinist and a singer, and I ended up giving her a couple of one-to-one violin lessons. I started to see a slow but definite change in her over the years—I witnessed her talking more freely to those people she knew, and she seemed to be generally happier in herself. After a while I could pinpoint why. It was clear to me that the music she wrote, along with the act of performing, gave her confidence and I was curious about what had triggered the change.

I don't pretend to be the sole cause of Catherine's improvement—I wouldn't be nearly so arrogant. It is difficult to put into words exactly how her story has informed mine, but the simplest explanation would be that working with her helped me to overcome some of my own anxieties. When I was having difficulty believing in myself, I managed to help another musician to believe in her own abilities and that gave me something to hold on to. She has been a constant figure in my musical journey.

If Catherine is a central character, then I can realistically call Rachel a plot point, albeit a very important one. Rachel was, I'm told, a violinist in one of the top orchestras in Wales and a tutor in composition, until she was involved in a horrific car accident that left her paralysed from the neck down. When I knew her she was confined to a wheelchair, but her brain worked perfectly and she had retained all of her musical knowledge. I had, I'll admit, no idea how we were going to get a composition from a woman who could not move, speak, or even wave a hand. I watched closely, desperately, for any reaction that I could grab on to, and when the suggestion was made of composing some light-hearted contemporary music, she scowled at us and then suddenly laughed. From then on I was determined to help her produce the best music she could. It was slow and laboured, and after a week of intense work we had perhaps a minute's worth of music. But when we performed it at the concert, Rachel's eyes lit up; I've never seen anyone look as full of joy as she did at that moment. I knew then that using music therapeutically, whatever it was and whatever it involved, was the right path for me. If music could help anyone as much as it had helped someone like her, then surely that was worth pursuing.

I ended up writing my final-year dissertation on the use of music therapy in young adults with developmental disabilities, for which, I'm proud to say, I achieved a first. During that year I also undertook a placement with Paul Whittaker's charity Music and the Deaf, conveniently based in Huddersfield. As well as working in the office, I assisted in music workshops at Doncaster College for the Deaf, and in rehearsals of the Hi-Notes ensemble, a group of hearing-impaired children who got together to perform music. Being the only person in that room who had full hearing capability (the musicians, composer and conductor were all deaf) was an experience I am not likely to forget—it is astonishing to think that, considering the piece changed in small ways every time it was performed, I am the only person in the world who has 'fully' heard that composition in that moment.

The end result of all this was my decision to train as a music therapist, and so the next stage of my journey is the MA in Music Therapy at Anglia Ruskin University in Cambridge, which I will be starting in September. In the past year, spent at home in between degrees, I have been volunteering at a special needs school which has provided me with some amazing experiences. This 'gap year' has for me been one of changes and discoveries, but my musical journey is far from over—there are always going to be new things to learn, new obstacles to overcome, and new challenges to undertake. I'm still having therapy for the anxiety and depression, and I'm learning to control it. I'm about ready to start my next chapter—the training. But I still have my first descant recorder; and a copy of *The Old Mole* stuck up on my wall.

Insights from the blind

Adam Ockelford

In one evening, my whole life changed.

It was the late 1970s. I was a student at the Royal Academy of Music in London, studying the oboe, piano, harpsichord and composition, and working for a BMus degree. My landlady's son, Paul (now Sir Paul) Ennals, worked at a school for the blind in Wimbledon called Linden Lodge and, having noticed how musical a number of the children appeared to be, had suggested that I might like to come along and meet them.

Having managed to put off the moment for a couple of weeks (I was somewhat wary of taking on something from which, I imagined—quite rightly—subsequent extrication would be difficult), I found myself in a small practice room with a boy called Anthony, who was about 11 or 12, I judged. He didn't seem to be able to see anything at all, and didn't turn to face me as we talked.

Paul had told me that Anthony played a number of instruments, including the drum kit, piano and saxophone, and that he learnt pieces entirely by ear—often after hearing them only once. Anthony had been assessed as having 'perfect pitch', by which they meant that when he heard a note, he knew exactly which one it was, without needing to test it out in relation to any others.

I asked Anthony what kind of music he liked, and whether he was fond of any particular composers. 'Frank Bridge', he replied immediately and then, after a pause, 'Franz Liszt'. At that, Anthony got up from the piano stool where he was sitting, apparently making room for me to sit down. Then it became clear what he wanted.

'B minor Sonata.'

Anthony was evidently a young man of few words, but they certainly packed a punch. I hesitated, thinking what to do. Surely he couldn't really expect me to play the whole sonata at the drop of a hat—and without the music too? There was an expectant silence. Doing nothing was not an option. Somewhat diffidently, my hands moved over the low Bs an octave apart with which the piece starts, and I managed to cobble together the opening bars of the sonata as best I could from memory. One or two of the notes may not have been quite as Liszt intended them.

It seemed to please Anthony, nonetheless, who flapped his hands with obvious pleasure.

Wind forward a week and—yes—I was back at Linden Lodge with Paul, heading along the music corridor to see Anthony once more. As we approached the practice room, Paul was just saying that Anthony had a piece he wanted to play to me when the unmistakable sound of the opening notes of the Liszt piano sonata started up. I couldn't help smiling—and my smile turned into a laugh as the piece continued complete with the errors that I had made last week. As we went into the room and greeted Anthony, he was clearly very amused too.

So, I was the butt of a clever musical joke from what was evidently an incisive young musical mind: here was someone who, for all his paucity of verbal expression, clearly revelled in musical communication. I was left wondering how many of my fellow students at the Academy would have been able to pull off such a feat—working entirely from a single hearing of the music.

But beyond this, a train of thought was set in motion that has occupied me ever since. How does the human mind, without any formal training, make sense of music? And, further to this, where did Anthony's exceptional musicality stem from? Were blind children typically more musical than their fully-sighted peers?

It was questions such as these that led me to undertake a PhD in music psychology at Goldsmith's College in London in the 1980s and early 1990s, and subsequently to become Professor of Music and Director of the Applied Music Research Centre at Roehampton University (with a spell in between as Director of Education at the Royal National Institute of Blind People, in London).

Over the years, I also became interested in children with autism, who often seemed to share many of the characteristics of those who were congenitally blind—not least a propensity to exceptional musical development—though often with highly idiosyncratic learning styles. And often, autism and blindness went hand in hand.

For example, there was Philip, aged eight, who was totally blind as a result of being born extremely premature. From an early age, Philip developed a keen interest in the works of J. S. Bach and, bar by bar, I taught him several of the preludes and fugues from the '48'. He was intrigued to work out how Bach would use one short theme over and over again, sometimes in inversion or augmentation. No-one made these arcane structures more transparent than the idiosyncratic Canadian pianist Glenn Gould, and Philip was particularly taken with his quirky interpretations, listening to the LPs (this was the 1980s) that I had given him, over and over again.

Philip was not without his eccentricities, too. One Friday, after several weeks of effort, he finished learning the ninth fugue from Book I of *The Well-Tempered Clavier*. He agreed to practise it complete over the weekend at home and perform it to me the following Monday. When the time came, we were both delighted with the result. The piece is demanding to play and had some awkward stretches for his small hands, but Philip had worked hard and he cleared most of the technical hurdles without stumbling. The fugue drew to an end, concluding on a sustained chord that Bach clearly intended as a moment of stasis at the climax of the piece. However, for some reason Philip saw fit to add another note in the left hand near the bottom of the keyboard after the winning post had been passed.

I congratulated him, for his playing had been as meticulous as ever. But I did ask what the extra 'E' at the end was for. There was an uncomfortable silence. I was perplexed. Evidently there was something going on here that I didn't understand. Philip must have known that the extra note wasn't in the original, and he liked to get things exactly right. Again, I asked him why he had done it. Once more he was evasive, though he finally muttered something about '735' making him unhappy. I felt that I was getting to understand less rather than more, and I asked him what he meant. He finally spat it out. 'It's an *odd number* and I don't like pieces with odd numbers of notes — so I added an extra one to make it alright.'

I wondered whether this was some kind of elaborate joke. I looked at him, sitting there earnestly on the piano stool — fingers pressing hard on his eyelids. I tried to think of an argument that would make sense to *him*. 'Presumably Bach *meant* the fugue to have an odd number of notes?' I asked, temporarily suspending my disbelief as to the composer's likely intentions. But it was to no avail. Philip was insistent that odd numbers of notes made him uncomfortable, and he just couldn't resist making them even. Could he *pretend* to play another note, I wondered — just listen to it in his head? No.

So in the end we compromised. From now on, in pieces with odd numbers of notes, Philip would add his extra one discreetly to a chord in the middle so that no-one else would notice.

Working over the years with many children like Philip, I learnt that autism is not one thing, but a spectrum of developmental disabilities that affect thinking, feeling and interaction with the environment and other people. Some people with autism function independently and engage freely in their choice of musical activities. Others find the world confusing: they may be unable to express themselves in words and find anything outside a familiar routine problematic. Relationships may be a particular source of anxiety. However, like blind children, their capacity to participate in musical activities may be unaffected, or even enhanced. A good deal of my recent research has been to consider why this should be the case.

I have come to the conclusion that most young children engage with sound in three different ways: as *speech*, as *music* and as a *feature of the environment*.

Some young children who are blind or autistic, though, seem to process many sounds, whatever their function, *as music*. This is because of:

- The *impact of blindness or autism* on the developing brain
- The *prevalence of music* in the environment
- The *way music is structured*

Although often regarded as the province of music therapy, there is no reason why a wide range of musicians should not work successfully with blind or autistic children and young people. Being empathetic and *interactive* is the key, and my advice to music teachers wishing to join me in this fascinating field is:

- Open your ears to the possibility that all sound can be heard as music; listen out for patterns and learn to relish repetition
- Interact through music *as though it were language*: imitate what children do, exactly at first, and then make changes; give them the sense that they are influencing *you*; offer fascinating musical fragments to copy; dialogue in sound; improvise simultaneously
- Support pupils in developing the technique they need to produce whatever they can hear in their heads on instruments or through singing: model the necessary movements for them; encourage them to attend to what you do by looking, listening and feeling; offer physical guidance

Why music?

Diane Paterson

I must have been about six. My friends down the road who were a bit older were all learning the recorder, and they came to my house to practise. I liked the sound and after they had gone I got hold of one of the books and worked my way through it, learning the notes and the notation from the clear instructions. It was the red recorder book that everyone used way back in those days. The recorders were wooden and went soggy after only a short while, becoming difficult to play. Later, when I played in a group in school, I hated it when it all buzzed when we weren't in tune with each other. There were two teachers who played the piano in my primary school. We thought one was much better than the other. One could play for music and movement, but the one we thought was better not only played in assembly but she could play *Jerusalem*. We were truly impressed. I remember wanting to be like both of them.

One girl from down my road went for piano lessons. My mother and I decided that I would go as well. My parents stumped up £10 to buy a second hand piano and I started to work my way through my grandfather's piano music before having any actual lessons. Having taught myself to read treble clef for the recorder I assumed bass clef was the same. (Once I realized it was only a third down it didn't take long to relearn it.) When I started lessons I didn't practise the piano pieces I was given by my teacher. I preferred my grandfather's harder pieces. I became a proficient sight reader.

One of my favourite memories is of my grandfather standing over me as I tackled the first movement of the *Moonlight Sonata*, telling me he was sure I could do it. Of course, not practising the exam pieces, I failed Grade 4. I was so cross with myself that I went on to get Grade 8 three years later, ploughing on through Grades 4 to 7 en route.

Inspirational teachers

Moving on to the Sixth Form, I became engrossed in everything to do with music. I was a church organist, I accompanied singing lessons, was in a jazz band, played for shows and even joined the local youth orchestra with my not so good Grade 4 violin playing. One A-level teacher told me someone the previous year got a B. I told him that that wouldn't be good enough for me, that I wanted an A, so I set to and read Grout's *History of Western Music* almost from cover to cover. I took my degree in Music at Leeds University, focusing on early music and palaeography and enjoying the discipline of editing early manuscripts.

I followed this with a PGCE at Reading University—what an amazing course. Arnold Bentley had just retired but he still led some seminars. He expounded the joys of using tonic sol-fa for promoting singing accurately and in tune. We weren't convinced then—I am now.

On day one we were given a brass instrument to learn to Grade 3 standard by the end of the year. That has been such a useful experience — to know how pupils can feel when presented with a new instrument — and such a great way to learn about brass instruments.

Each Wednesday afternoon they introduced us to a different teaching method or approach: Dalcroze, Kodály, Orff, Avril Dankworth (teaching many different ways of playing one tune), Brain Bonsor (on recorder ensembles), John Paynter (on creative music). All were truly inspirational. At my first job I could use almost none of it (except the recorder ensembles) — there was almost no room for creative music or even classroom percussion. It was all listening, writing about listening, or singing.

Sudden change of direction

I was teaching music at a local high school when my husband Stuart became suddenly ill, an operation followed and he suffered brain damage. With my two children, aged three years and six months in tow, I decided that my husband might be able to communicate with me through music — not that he was a musician. I took a small keyboard into the hospital, and with what was left of his strength he could sometimes play the sounds.

After he died I searched for ways of working with people who had brain damage, leading a music listening course in a local hospital. Whilst working there I met Adele Drake of Drake Music fame. Out of curiosity, I visited her workshop where Andrew Cleaton was exploring ways of composing using computers. I had never seen so much technology in one room and had no idea what any of it did, but the sessions were inspirational and very exciting. I became a volunteer and eventually co-ran the workshops when Andrew was away. I still remember the first time I switched on a computer myself. It was 1992 and it was an Atari. I was surprised that I found music technology reasonably easy to understand and loved the possibilities it opened up for people with disabilities. We worked with prototype sound beams and other new MIDI controllers including an early version of MIDIcreator and added in various drum pads and microphones with effect units. I became involved with a design project at York University Electronic Music Department, testing Tim Anderson's new accessible software which could enable people to control the computer and compose with just one or two switches. I surprised myself by driving to meetings at York University Physics Department as a member of the Ensemble Research Group, which looked at how new musical instruments could be created using this new technology.

I moved from the Drake Music Project to Leeds Music Support Service, becoming a peripatetic music teacher for pupils with special needs. This proved to be a steep learning curve. For the first time, I met pupils on the severe end of the autistic spectrum and children with severe learning difficulties who didn't appear to be interested in their surroundings or in me. Both groups would respond well to music — especially singing and the accordion. I discovered I had an ability to interact musically with many of these pupils. Perhaps it is a similar process to accompanying.

In this new job I needed to learn how to work with pupils who were blind and visually impaired, deaf and hearing impaired, or on the autistic spectrum. I would scour staff-room notice boards and journals for information on the latest thinking about how to communicate with pupils who are difficult to reach. I went on all the courses I could find, including some led by Sally Zimmerman, Claus Bang and Wendy Prevezer, and learned Stage 1 sign language. I was greatly supported and also inspired by the work of the Yorkshire Association for Music and Special Educational Needs (YAMSEN), especially the evening workshops run by Mavis West and Jan Holdstock.

I found I was now able to use all the different approaches to music teaching which I'd been introduced to on my PGCE course. There had been very little opportunity for using them in mainstream secondary schools, but now they formed the core of my work. The presence of a network of interested teachers created by YAMSEN meant that together we could explore new ideas and rework old ones. Over the last 15 years we have developed multi-sensory musical activity days which enable children with Profound and Multiple Learning Difficulties to experience live music through the use of fabrics and props, using ideas which I began to realize had their origin in Dalcroze. I went to the summer school to find out more.

I followed this up by attending a Voices Foundation five-day course which developed my knowledge of the Kodály method. I've found this to be an effective way into communication with many children who have very little language. Songs based on just three notes are so easy for them to understand and to join in with—even if they are only vocalizing.

I went on the Orff Summer School to find out how this approach fitted in and discovered that this was in many ways the key to the structure of musical learning, bringing together many different threads that I had learned and been practising over the years.

Latterly schools in our area have shown more interest in music technology, which was not the case when I got this job in 1996. I am now able to use the skills I learned when working with the Drake Music Project and have set up a room with the technology embedded in it, as well as having kits that we can take into schools. One privilege of working for Drake was attending the inspirational Share Music Summer Schools. The Surrey one was led by Richard Stilgoe. You arrived at the beginning of the week with a blank sheet and by the end you and your group had composed music to tell a part of a story which you performed in a production on the last night. It was a challenge to everyone's creativity and a model we are sometimes able to replicate in a small way on projects in school and in our new sound and light room.

However, it wasn't just the use of technology that I discovered at Share Music. Their centre in Lisnaskea in Northern Ireland had a gamelan. I didn't know what this was when I arrived there. The course that summer was led by Daryl Runswick and Mary King and the music combined jazz ideas with the sounds of the new gamelan which had been bought for its accessibility for children with special needs. That experience led me to want to buy our own gamelan—which we now have.

Lastly I have to mention music therapy. I often get called the 'singing lady'—or sometimes the 'music therapist'. I am neither of these. But I do think it essential to be able to offer music therapy in our city. This way of working appears to me to pull together many of the musical and non-musical interactions that teachers use in schools. We find we need to inform local schools what music therapy is. It's not piano or drumming lessons—it's about communication. But if you are to work with children with special needs, I've discovered that you need to understand the process which music therapists use and learn from their methods and interactive approach.

The work with children with special needs continues to be a challenge. The thinking never stands still. We are always exploring new ways of working. Throughout it all, our goal is always to reach the children—they are the true source of our inspiration.

The formative four

Vanessa Richards

I was desperate to play the flute when I was aged around seven, only to find it wasn't taught at primary school—they only taught the violin. I started to learn, but then a friend suggested I might like to spend my weekends in a marching band and the only instrument small enough for me to hold and walk with at the same time (as I was somewhat small) was a cornet. It seemed like a fun idea and so I became probably one of the smallest cornet players in the Derbyshire marching band circuit, ably taught by the bandmaster Colin. My absolute defining moment was when a relative who used to play the clarinet with the Black Watch prior to World War II took me to see the Hallé Orchestra play Holst's *The Planets* at the Royal Concert Hall in Nottingham. From that moment I knew I wanted to be a musician. I was smitten.

When I reached secondary school I could only have free lessons on one instrument. By that time I was much better at the trumpet so carried on with that. I had my first 'proper' instrumental lesson with the renowned (although I didn't know it at the time) brass teacher and brass band conductor Steve Shimwell. He took me through to Grade 8 by the time I was 14 and I played in his brass bands up to the time I went to Sixth Form. I also played with the County Youth Orchestra, and the same relative who took me to my first concert came to almost every concert I played in. Into his nineties now, he still tries to come along if I'm playing and never fails to ask how it went.

Steve Shimwell was a big influence on my playing, and brass bands continue to be my favourite ensembles to play in. They seem to embody so many good things about musical life that I try to instill in my pupils: the pleasure of playing with others, the teamwork required and the sheer satisfaction of a job well done. I have never failed to perform in a concert, where I thank my lucky stars I can use my skills to create such emotion.

My secondary school teacher, Mrs Saunders, was also a big influence. She would drive me around Derbyshire regularly to go to concerts, performances, exams and auditions. She was so generous with her time—something I'm sure influenced in some way my own decision to teach music. Music teaching does not often fit to a sociable timetable but the rewards are huge. She was a great believer in 'making learning relevant'. We all used to pay a penny towards a weekly single (yes—it was still records then) and then every week each class would vote for their favourite chart song. Mrs Saunders would then disappear off to buy a single for every class. We always imagined her tripping off to the shops with about 20 bags of 1p coins. I'm sure she didn't, but it always made us laugh to think of her. I only remember one of these records—it was a Duran Duran single but I cannot remember which. She taught us *Hey Jude* and the strange thing is that one of my classes this year requested that very same song, which is obviously still relevant for them.

During my O-level year there were only three of us in the group. One of our study works was Bartók's *Mikrokosmos*. Mrs Saunders knew nothing about it and could find no recording, so went off to buy a copy of the sheet music and spent all the summer learning some of the pieces. The first time I heard it was an absolute treat. Contemporary music was a new phenomenon to us and the three of us sat wide eyed and dumbstruck. Her only comment after the playing was, 'Hmm . . . interesting, what do you think?' I can still hear the question in my head whenever I hear this music. I'm still amazed she asked our opinion so early on.

When I went to Huddersfield Polytechnic I continued along the brass band route and was taught variously by Colin Casson, David James and Phil McCann. I played for Hammonds Sauce Works Band at the time they won the National Brass Championships in 1989. I loved the variety of experiences and backgrounds we all had. I loved the fact that you could always hear music, whatever time of day you were in the building. When I taught in primary schools my classroom was still like that; there was always music playing. I loved being able to introduce new music, music for different times of the day, music for different events—it was a great joy.

How I made it into teaching I'm not quite sure. I'm not even sure I always wanted to teach although, as I said before, Mrs Saunders was a big part of that decision, so it maybe came about during my later secondary years. In the end I decided against music teaching and went for primary school teaching. It was during my time as a primary teacher that I met one of the best teachers of music I've ever met, Mr Batey. He was not the traditional musician, having a degree in, I think, sound engineering—but his teaching of music was just a joy to watch. He had such passion for the subject and his grasp of technology put us all to shame. The times we worked together on musical events and productions were some of the most memorable I have had. He spent an amazing amount of time trying to learn the piano and managed to progress to Grade 3.

Now I've probably got the perfect job. I still teach the primary-age group, but now only music—all day every day. I still try to follow the influences of my early life—my relative's belief in the power of live music, Steve Shimwell's belief in the power of hard work, Mrs Saunders' belief in the relevance to the child and Mr Batey's passion for the subject. The four of them together probably sum up my philosophy very well. What a legacy they left me, and I thank them all.

So, what may the future hold? In this world of uncertainty it is hard to know. I've continued to study and gained my MA in Music; I've continued to teach music to the best of my ability; and I hope I will continue to live by my philosophy through any challenges which come my way. Where we as music teachers will be in five years is difficult to predict. Where I myself will be is somewhat easier. I'll still be playing my trumpet and my piano, I'll still be listening to live music, I'll still be passionate about music and I hope I'll still have the opportunity to pass that passion on to the next generation.

At 18 I failed my A-levels, on Friday Paul McCartney will give me my Masters Degree—what music has done for me

Alison Richardson

I cannot remember learning to read music, but I do remember playing recorder with my mum and sister. I also remember singing little tunes to myself and asking my mum if I was good at music. She replied yes. This might have been a genuine response or the reaction of a parent trying to silence an annoying seven-year-old. Whatever the reason for this answer, I will be forever grateful for it as it gave me the self-belief that has carried me on my musical path and into my career. I always knew I would be a music teacher as music was the only thing I was good at in school, and I did not think I was good enough as a player to do that professionally.

I decided I wanted to play a brass instrument after hearing a local music centre concert that my parents had taken me to see. I joined a local youth band and started to learn to play the cornet. Unfortunately, the band soon folded and I lost this opportunity to play. However, when I went to primary school I had to take the Bentley test and, as a result, I was given a violin and began to learn to play. I do not have the personality of a violinist, and after getting 100 in my Grade 2, the violin and I parted company. At the end of my first year of secondary school I found myself without an instrument.

Fortunately, the secondary school I went to had an excellent Saturday morning music centre and I was able to pick up a penny whistle and join the Crabapple Ceilidh Band. I was not diagnosed as dyslexic until I was at music college, and I found school difficult as I was labelled as a bit thick and lazy (to be fair I was a bit lazy). Playing with Crabapple kept me engaged with school. The leader of, and inspiration behind, Crabapple was folk musician and geography teacher, John Reay. He was an amazing person and I am indebted to him for what he did for me. I remember music at Wyndham School as being vibrant in those days, thanks to the music teachers such as Sarah Kekus and Chris Howarth. In my third year I was encouraged to join another brass band and I started playing cornet again. I am grateful to my cornet teacher, Simon Yeo, who was patient with me as I did little practice. However, I was playing six times a week with various bands and orchestras and, with his excellent teaching, I achieved my Grade 8.

I did not do so well in the classroom and finished Sixth Form with no A-levels and no place at university. Assuming I would get the one E grade I needed to take up the offer of a place at Newcastle Polytechnic, my parents had gone on holiday the week of A-level results, so there was a bit of a panic as we tried to organize my future. From their holiday cottage my parents trawled the papers looking for universities offering places (no computers to do this in those days) and they noticed Leeds Music College had places left on their diploma course. Within a week and a half I had auditioned, got a place, been to Reading Music Festival, found somewhere to live and moved down to Leeds.

Leeds was a revelation to me, and it was very exciting to be involved in such a vibrant music scene. Studying here gave me the opportunity to play with some great people in some great venues including the Barbican in London. However, all these opportunities still did not inspire me to work very hard or do much practice and I was continuing to do just enough to get by. It was my Alexander Technique teacher who first mentioned the subject of dyslexia. I went for a test which confirmed that I was, in fact, dyslexic. From here things started to look up as I began to understand why things seemed harder for me than for others. I passed my Diploma in Leeds and went to Cardiff to study on a two-year BA (Hons) course in Music Education. I was getting support with my education now, working harder and enjoying the feeling of achievement. I enjoyed teaching very much and finished my degree with a 2:1.

I have been teaching now for 15 years and I am Head of Department and Curriculum Leader for the Arts at a large secondary school. Education has been demystified for me now, and when I work hard I get results. I enjoy learning as much as teaching and I recently finished a part-time MA at the Liverpool Institute for Performing Arts. This Masters Degree in Performing Arts Education included a dissertation that explored the question: 'Can using the secondary benefits of music education in learning objectives improve engagement in Year 7 music lessons?' My research involved placing learning objectives for transferable skills alongside the music learning objectives, and introducing methods of differentiation other than cognitive complexity. I also allowed time for the students to reflect on their learning through their own written narratives.

In other words, I wanted to show that developing creative approaches would engage students and encourage independent learning. I believe that giving students a skills-based learning objective goes some way towards putting the child at the heart of the education process. Doing this makes the lessons more student-centred whilst maintaining the integrity of the music curriculum. This in turn recognizes that the value of studying music is not the same for each student. My view is that the importance of studying music lies in music for music's sake as an important art form. However, it should be recognized that there are other benefits to studying music and, if exploiting these can help engage students in music lessons so that they can access the aesthetic side of music, then this must be beneficial to music education. If this in turn then encourages students to partake in extra-curricular music-making, perhaps music education will benefit society as a whole.

My MA studies have enriched and informed my teaching, and have really changed the way I regard the educational process. I am very excited by the new perspective I have, which allows me to make a difference both to the students I teach and to the staff I lead. As teachers, we have the opportunity not just to provide our students with knowledge for life, but also to develop in them the skills which they can draw on to live productive and fulfilling lives, enriching the school and the community they live in.

I am grateful that I always knew what path I would follow, as this stopped me from giving up when I failed at things. I look back on my music education now and wish I had sung more, practised more and started the piano earlier. However, whatever my wishes for my past, I would not change a single thing about where I am now.

Music to the ear

Paul Whittaker

Music was always around in the house when I was growing up, something I feel is true of most deaf children of hearing parents. The child may not know that this force is actually called 'music', but will be aware that it affects people in powerful ways.

When I was five I wanted to learn the piano, but trying to find a teacher was tricky. Admittedly, prospective teachers would not be filled with confidence when they received this call from my mother: 'Hello. My son would love to learn the piano. Unfortunately he can't hear what he's playing and he can't hear what you're saying to him because he's profoundly deaf. Interested?' Despite this, I did find a teacher quite quickly and began doing ABRSM exams soon afterwards.

A couple of years later I joined my local church choir, Holy Trinity, Huddersfield. I firmly believe that being in a choir when young is one of the best music experiences you can get. You have the fun of being part of a group, learn to sight-read music quickly (surprisingly, I'm rubbish at learning by ear) and sing a wide range of music.

Through the choir, I became interested in the organ and began learning when I was 12 with Jonathan Bielby at Wakefield Cathedral. Round about the same time I decided that I wanted to get a music degree and then find some way of helping deaf people, and those who live and work with them, to enjoy music. Initially I had the idea of having some kind of mansion, where people could come for courses and from which the staff could go out and about leading workshops. Obviously, I had little idea then of the potential cost of such a venture and of all the legislation involved, but I have ended up doing what I dreamed of all those years ago through Music and the Deaf.

Although my various organ and piano teachers—Margaret Braithwaite, Frank Wardle, Winifred Smith and Keith Jarvis—taught me a huge amount, if I had to pick just one person who inspired me most it would have to be Hedley Teale. He was the music teacher at Belle Vue Boys' School, Bradford, and he was also very involved in the local music scene. His passion for music was just so infectious and he never saw my deafness as a barrier at all.

Partly because I did come up against discrimination when I was younger, I suppose I've become a passionate believer in looking for people's *abilities*, not their *disabilities*. I certainly felt discriminated against when I tried to get into university, and 12 different ones turned me down over two years due to my deafness. At one point it felt like I would never be accepted anywhere, so I'll always be grateful to Wadham College, Oxford, and to Edward Olleson, my tutor in the Music Faculty, for accepting me when I applied there. To be honest, I didn't think I was clever enough for Oxbridge, but had three wonderful years at Wadham before spending a year at the Royal Northern College of Music doing a post-graduate organ course.

By 1988 I was, in theory, a mature, handsome, intelligent music graduate and had to decide what to do with my life. Enter Music and the Deaf—the only job I've ever had and probably will ever have. It began in my attic at my parents' house with me as the sole worker and even now, 23 years later, it's still a very small team that runs it—Danny Lane (full time), Tina Johnstone (part-time administrator) and me.

Through the years, Music and the Deaf (MatD) has run many projects but at present we're focused mainly on just two. For the past five years we've run a Deaf Youth Orchestra in West Yorkshire and since the start of 2011 have been developing this more widely. To date we've set up similar groups in the North West of England, London and the East of England. Over the next few years we hope to set up many more so that we eventually cover the whole of the UK and can establish a National Deaf Youth Orchestra. Inevitably, we do require a lot of funding for this, along with a large number of tutors, leaders and regional co-ordinators. Few deaf children get the opportunity to learn to play an instrument, never mind being able to meet and play with other young people who are also deaf, so this is a valuable and worthwhile project. The response from players, parents, tutors and audiences is overwhelmingly positive and many people do tell us that what we do 'changes people's lives'.

Being told this is very humbling. We didn't set out with that aim but are increasingly aware that this is indeed the case. Being able to encourage deaf children to end their isolation, and to give parents and families hope whilst enabling them all to share in the joy of making music is a wonderful thing. We know that we're all very fortunate to work for MatD.

The other main project concerns signed song, which is something I've been involved in for many years, but this really took off when MatD became a Sing Up Flagship organization. Over the past four years we've run various courses and created numerous resources to enable both deaf and hearing people to join together through singing and signing. One of the real attractions of signed song is that it gives you a far deeper understanding of what you're singing about and it's such a fantastic feeling for me to see large groups of people come together and do it. As with the orchestras, we do have plans to develop regional and national signing choirs and will be creating more resources to enable this.

Signed song has led me into other, new and exciting areas of work. In 2010 I was privileged to be asked to sign the first ever signed Prom, *Sondheim at 80*. As a classical musician you dream of taking part in the Proms but I never expected that I would do so, especially in front of Sondheim himself and performing with Dame Judi Dench. Four weeks after that I found myself at Edinburgh International Festival signing Opera Lyon's production of *Porgy and Bess*. Through that job I've recently been to Paris to film some signed sections of *The Rite of Spring* for a commission at the Turku Festival in Finland. And in 2011 I'm back at the Proms and Edinburgh, for *Horrible Histories* and Rossini's opera *Semiramide* respectively.

Looking back, I know I'm a really lucky fella. I spend my whole life doing what I enjoy most, which is making music and being able to share it with others. I've met some amazing people, worked with some of the best musicians on the planet, and I'm still only 47. Yet, without my hearing aids, I can't hear a thing and rely entirely on the printed score in order to understand any piece of music. But then, music's not about your hearing but about your whole being—what you feel, what you see, what you express. I cannot imagine life without music and would urge you, whatever your ability or disability, to make it, enjoy it and share it with whoever you can and wherever you can. Even with those who (allegedly) can't hear it.

Section 4

Da Capo

Rivers of Musical Experience: a tool for reflecting and researching individual pathways

Pamela Burnard

This chapter explores a research and reflection tool called 'Rivers of Musical Experience' which can help us to represent, construct and reconstruct significant milestones or events in our musical learning journeys. It also considers what we can learn from others' reflections on and about their individual musical pathways.

As musicians, music teachers and learners have to take the simple but all important step of using unusual, even new, tools for reflection; instruments without sharp edges but with a powerful zoom lens that will give authentic insights into our own (and our students') learning journeys. Critical incident charting—adapted and referred to here as 'Rivers of Musical Experience'—refers to one such tool that has been used in counselling and psychotherapy, educational research and teacher education.

Critical incident charting originated as a clinical tool used in Personal Construct Psychology (Kelly, 1955/1991) and was later developed, alongside other labels, as 'career-rivers' by education researchers (e.g. Denicolo & Pope, 1990; Pope & Denicolo, 1993, 1997). The term 'critical incident', however, has been used widely in the research literature on classroom teachers and indeed has a long tradition in ethnographies of other cultures. In many cases, its use has been synonymous with periods of strain, beginnings and endings of teachers' careers, and turning points that are brought about by surprise or shock (Woods, 1993; Tripp, 1993; Prosser, 1998). The path to understanding what we do and why we do it is through reflecting and acting on those reflections.

There are several types of critical phase that mark times of change and choosing. For example, 'extrinsic' phases include historical events, conditions that force decisions or act as obstacles. 'Intrinsic' phases usually involve a natural progression of a career, whilst 'personal' phases bring to the forefront particular issues relating to, for example, family. In relation to detailed charting of classroom teaching, the critical incident does not necessarily introduce anything new into the practices of the teacher, but rather acts to crystallize ideas, attitudes and beliefs, which are already being formed. A critical incident may create a turning point, which is confirmed by a subsequent 'counter incident'. For example, with Figure 4 below, the 'critical incident' of failing a practical challenge at university prompted a 'counter incident' of rethinking her future profession as a teacher rather than professional performer.

Introducing 'Rivers of Musical Experience': a critical incident charting tool

In my own research, I have adapted the use of critical incident charting for reflecting on experience of a particular musical phenomenon (Burnard, 2000a, 2000b, 2004) and as a means for researching aspects of teacher identity (Burnard, 2003a, 2003b) and of children's and adults' musical creativities (2006a, 2006b, 2008, 2011, 2012). This reflective tool has also been used to capture the secondary school teacher's musical career paths (Odena & Welch, 2007), life histories of instrumental and vocal teachers (Baker, 2005), reflections of pre-service teachers (Kerchner, 2006), and to trace the musical lives of mature-age keyboard players (Taylor, 2011).

During interviews, or on sheets of paper, respondents annotate a winding timeline with key turning points, critical incidents or significant episodes. As a tool for reflection, creating 'Rivers of Musical Experience' encourages active involvement from participants in an emancipatory and democratic way. Like rivers, the words start to flow since the participants draw them in ways that they own and that they feel are appropriate.

The following examples are drawn from diverse research projects that examine musical learning. They show the use of three different methods of critical incident charting:

- Participant self-report charting: participants write down specific instances that they consider have influenced the direction of their outlook. (See Figures 1 and 2 below, constructed by student teachers.)
- Interviewer/researcher charting: the researcher uses an interview to construct a chart or 'river' which is then verified or adapted by the interviewee. (See Figures 3 and 4, from practising teachers.)
- Interviewee-interviewer charting: where a narrative is co-constructed around incidents that both interviewee and interviewer consider highly influential. (See Figures 5 and 6, from a secondary age student.)

Student Teachers' Musical Pathways

We can compare (see Figures 1 and 2) the contrasting experiences at each bend in the winding rivers of these two primary student teachers, neither of them a music specialist, and consider how the factors of musical opportunity and socialization influence their level of confidence about teaching music in school.

In initial teacher training courses, we hear many musically traumatic stories involving highly charged incidents from early school days in which personal and professional identities are invested. These anecdotes are well supported by a growing body of evidence that suggests negative experiences can have a significant influence on musical ability and restrict the majority to become procurers of rather than producers of music. As their lecturer and tutor, this gives me a profound insight into each student's thinking before we even come to interact personally and professionally in class.

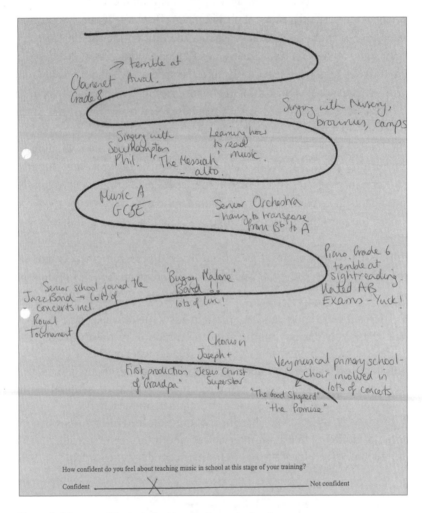

Figure 1: More confident student teacher's musical pathway

In these two examples we witness how positive and negative critical incidents lead to positive and negative musical identities. By examining such incidents, therefore, we gain insight into the processes by which identities are built by individuals at particular points in their lives. This in turn provokes a series of further choices and challenges.

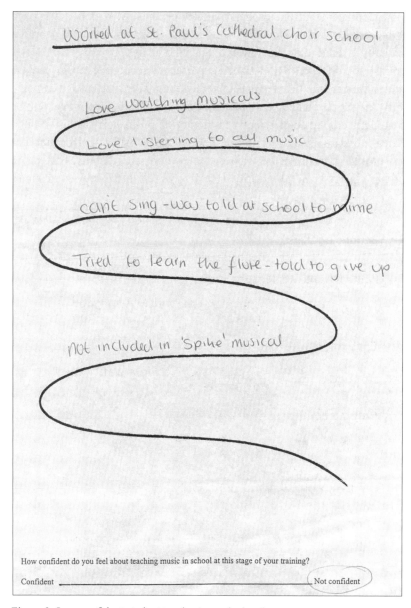

Figure 2: Less confident student teacher's musical pathway

Experienced Music Teachers' Musical Pathways

This point is further evidenced in the 'Musical River' of a primary generalist music teacher with two years' teaching experience (see Figure 3), whose straightforward yet powerful musical life history shows how he came from a family where the parents had neither musical interest nor skill but recognized the importance of providing children with opportunities for musical learning. Although this teacher did not perceive himself as possessing the same level of musicianship as others, he relied solely on encouragement from teachers to develop a musical identity that consequently enabled him to develop musically. Having at one time announced to people who he professionally wanted to *be,* he now explains who he has *become.*

In contrast, Figure 4 sees a mid-career, experienced secondary music teacher reflect on the milestones or significant events in her learning journey. Her journey begins with her family, the support and development of performance and the movement between how meaning is embodied differently in the notion of musician with its foundations and realization at the centre of all that she values, which is performing. The key incidents provide a basis for her values, motivations and identity. For this teacher, 'Playing has always been my priority. I've always felt that I've been destined along

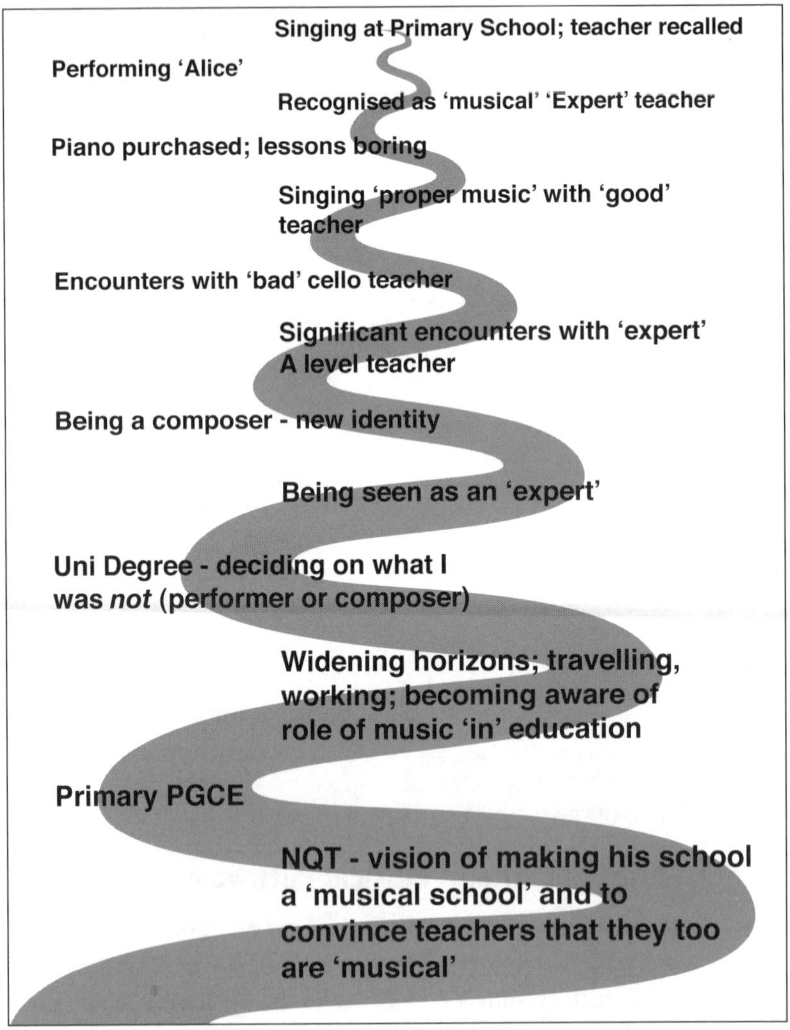

Singing at Primary School; teacher recalled

Performing 'Alice'

Recognised as 'musical' 'Expert' teacher

Piano purchased; lessons boring

Singing 'proper music' with 'good' teacher

Encounters with 'bad' cello teacher

Significant encounters with 'expert' A level teacher

Being a composer - new identity

Being seen as an 'expert'

Uni Degree - deciding on what I was *not* (performer or composer)

Widening horizons; travelling, working; becoming aware of role of music 'in' education

Primary PGCE

NQT - vision of making his school a 'musical school' and to convince teachers that they too are 'musical'

Figure 3: An early career primary music teacher's musical pathway

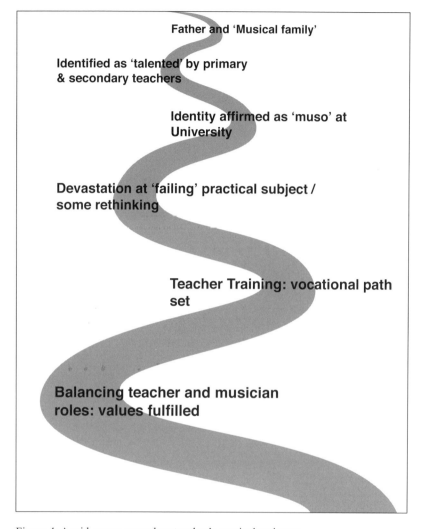

Figure 4: A mid-career secondary teacher's musical pathway

this musical path and maybe the teaching path . . . the musical path certainly since a young age.'

The complexity of the factors that shape musical identities is recognized in both these winding rivers in which each participant goes far beyond the simple invitation to share stories. With 'Musical Rivers' we gain an insight into the processes by which identities are built for individuals at particular points in their learning journeys, with what is important placed in the forefront. This type of charting of people's descriptions of their own individual pathways or learning journeys shows how we endow certain fundamental experiences with meaning and give them a prominent location in our explanations of our musical selves.

A secondary student's developing musical pathway

This complexity is seen in the musical pathway expressed by Sidin at age 12 and then four years later, at age 16.

Figure 5 shows Sidin at 12, a girl with no formal training on an instrument and no instruments at home, whose negative musical identity and perceived absence of musical ability can be tracked in key moments in her musical life. For this young person, making statements like these suggest that, despite her musical enthusiasm, being 'musical' is an attribute she does not see in herself.

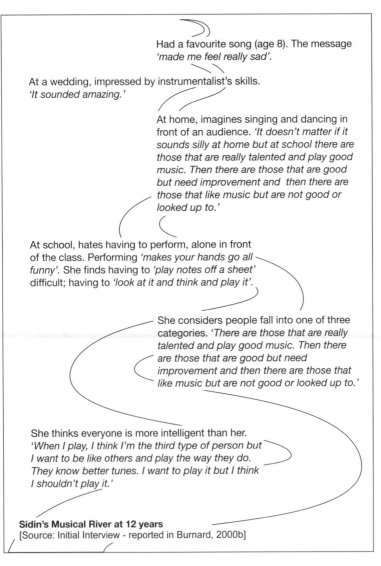

Had a favourite song (age 8). The message *'made me feel really sad'*.

At a wedding, impressed by instrumentalist's skills. *'It sounded amazing.'*

At home, imagines singing and dancing in front of an audience. *'It doesn't matter if it sounds silly at home but at school there are those that are really talented and play good music. Then there are those that are good but need improvement and then there are those that like music but are not good or looked up to.'*

At school, hates having to perform, alone in front of the class. Performing *'makes your hands go all funny'*. She finds having to *'play notes off a sheet'* difficult; having to *'look at it and think and play it'*.

She considers people fall into one of three categories. *'There are those that are really talented and play good music. Then there are those that are good but need improvement and then there are those that like music but are not good or looked up to.'*

She thinks everyone is more intelligent than her. *'When I play, I think I'm the third type of person but I want to be like others and play the way they do. They know better tunes. I want to play it but I think I shouldn't play it.'*

Sidin's Musical River at 12 years
[Source: Initial Interview - reported in Burnard, 2000b]

Figure 5: Sidin's musical pathway at age 12

The perceived barriers to Sidin's involvement in music continue, as conveyed in Figure 6 where, at age 16, Sidin explains,

> Music is for me something of a damaged dream really. I just lost the opportunity at secondary school. I met with friends who weren't really into music. Now, I'm really busy with coursework and homework. I haven't got time. I have to stick with being scared of doing things with music in front of people.

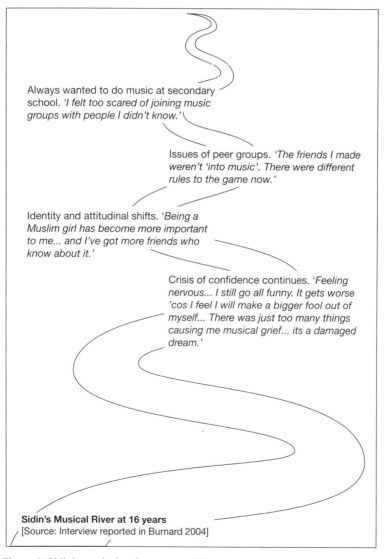

Figure 6: Sidin's musical pathway at age 16

For this anxious adolescent, her learning journey and identity were inextricably linked, providing a deeper understanding of the need to chart and relate to the musical lives of our students.

So, what else can 'Rivers of Musical Experience' tell us?

Every account involves a set of claims about oneself. For me personally, it was a tool that illuminated the trajectory of my career in a way that set me off on a path of reflection on particular phases, making sense—often for the first time—of choices taken and preferences made, which subsequently involved a reassessment of my priorities.

I used this tool to engage in reflection about my own beliefs when I moved into teacher education. I needed to see how the reflective process translated into my own teaching. The effect has been to develop the ability to adapt and change according to context, understanding events from the perspective of others, whilst retaining a sense of self. And this is precisely the way in which the critical incident works.

Similarly, for my student teachers, this is a tool that helps to crystallize ideas, attitudes and beliefs, many of which may have previously been held unconsciously. The effect of reflecting on critical phases in a life story, or critical periods within a career or a particular school placement, is far reaching. By engaging in this process we can effect change in ourselves and others by highlighting the specific issues that determine how we as teachers and learners come to perceive ourselves and others.

For me, becoming cognisant of the critical importance of early musical experiences on the development of children's musical abilities and identities has involved both rethinking the nature of our profession in music and music education and also making a commitment to broadening awareness of what constitutes everyone's innate musicality. As Blacking envisioned, we need to 'show that human beings are even more remarkable than we presently believe them to be—and not just a few human beings, but all human beings' (1976: 116).

Summary: How can 'Musical Rivers' be used?

We can use 'Musical River' charting to

- Reflect on beliefs about teaching and learning by identifying critical moments in our lives and the strength of emotion attached to those moments
- Reflect on why and how our thinking has changed, by identifying patterns and particular sequences of events in our teaching, development or career paths
- Examine who we are teaching and what they are thinking
- Help our students to examine what shapes them, how bits of their lives link together and how they feel about aspects of their experience that might not normally be accessible to them
- Reflect on the model teacher and the teaching model and how expert teachers view themselves

- Understand children's musical values, attitudes, beliefs, and multiple experiences so the meanings we make truly represent children's culture

Finding out what our students know, feel and think about what they know and do requires attending very carefully to them and respecting their abilities, backgrounds and beliefs. In order to do this we need to help our students tell their stories; illuminate the general relationships among their musical lives, training and careers; and help them seek self-reflection, self-enquiry and self-knowledge. This will ensure their many selves are realized, their voices heard and identities celebrated.

Using 'Musical Rivers' has profoundly influenced my own teaching. I have discovered how the reflection process can act as an antidote to the 'expected outcomes' of government schemes and benchmarks. That I am constantly inspired, refreshed, renewed and more often *changed with and by* my students is testament to the catalytic way in which the act of reflection, as a shared act, provokes thought and demands action. With increasing emphasis on accountability in teaching, we can no longer afford to regard our role as anything else but professional. To become agents of change requires the greatest of professionalism, expertise and respect.

References

Baker, D. (2005) Music service teachers' life histories in the United Kingdom with implications for practice. *International Journal of Music Education*, 23(3): 263–277.

Blacking, J. (1976) *How musical is man?* London: Faber.

Burnard, P. (2000a) Examining experiential differences between improvisation and composition in children's music-making. *British Journal of Music Education*, 17(3): 227–245.

Burnard, P. (2000b) How children ascribe meaning to improvisation and composition: rethinking pedagogy in music education. *Music Education Research*, 2(1): 7–23.

Burnard, P. (2003a) How musical are you? Examining the discourse of derision in music education. In S. Leong (ed.) *Musicianship in the 21st century: Issues, trends and possibilities.* International Society of Music Education (ISME), University of Western Australia Press.

Burnard, P. (2003b) *Becoming music teachers: Critical phases and career paths compared.* Paper given at the Third International Conference of Research in Music Education (RIME) Exeter, 8–11 April.

Burnard, P. (2004) Adolescent realities and changing perspectives on school music. In P. Shand (ed.). *Music education entering the 21st century.* International Society of Music Education (ISME), University of Western Australia Press.

Burnard, P. (2006a) The individual and social worlds of children's creativity. In G. McPherson (ed.) *The child as musician* (pp. 353–375). Oxford: Oxford University Press.

Burnard, P. (2006b) Understanding children's meaning-making as composers. In I. Deliège and G. Wiggins (eds.) *Musical creativity: Multidisciplinary research in theory and practice* (pp. 146–167). New York: Psychology Press.

Burnard, P. (2008) A phenomenological study of music teachers' approaches to inclusive education practices among disaffected youth. *Research Studies in Music Education,* 30(1): 59–76.

Burnard, P. (2011) Rethinking musical creativity. In O. Odena (ed.) *Musical creativity: Insights from music education research.* Aldershot, Hants: Ashgate.

Burnard, P. (2012 forthcoming/in press) *Musical creativities in real world practice.* Oxford: Oxford · University Press.

Denicolo, P. & Pope, M. (1990) Adults learning—Teachers thinking. In C. Day, M. Pope & P. Denicolo (eds.) *Insight into teachers thinking and practice.* London: Falmer.

Kelly, G.A. (1955/1991) *The psychology of personal constructs* (2 vols). London: Routledge.

Kerchner, J. (2006) Using reflective tools for teaching in arts education. In P. Burnard & S. Hennessy, S. (eds.) *Reflective practices in arts education.* Dordrecht: Springer.

Odena, O. & Welch, G. (2007) The influence of teachers' backgrounds on their perceptions of musical creativity. A qualitative study with secondary school music teachers. *Research Studies in Music Education,* 28: 71–81.

Pope, M. & Denicolo, P. (1993) The art and science of constructivist research in teacher thinking. *Teacher and Teacher Education*, 9(5/6): 529–544.

Pope, M. & Denicolo, P. (1997) (eds.) *Sharing understanding and practice.* Farnborough: European Personal Construct Association Publications.

Prosser, J. (1998) (ed.) *Image-based research: A sourcebook for qualitative researchers.* London: Falmer.

Taylor, A. (2011) Continuity, change and mature musical identity construction: Using 'Rivers of Musical Experience' to trace the musical lives of six mature-age keyboard players. *British Journal of Music Education*, 28(2): 195–212.

Tripp, D. (1993) *Critical incidents in teaching: Developing professional judgement.* London: Routledge.

Woods, P. (1993) *Critical events in teaching and learning.* London: Falmer.

Afterword

If you have been inspired by reading this book, you may like to reflect on your own musical pathway by constructing your own 'River of Musical Experience' using Pamela Burnard's technique, as described below.

An invitation to chart your own 'River of Musical Experience'

- Visualize your musical life as a winding river in which each bend in the river's path marks a critical moment. Think back and reflect on key moments (positive and negative memories) that have influenced the direction of your musical life. What are the first most significant memories, persons, events or pivotal moments that you recall about your musical journey (or your development as a teacher)?

- Locate each important episode on a different bend along the length of a winding river where each bend represents a critical moment or turning point. Tell the story (or recall it in your mind) of this important episode. Label the episode (e.g. 'Singing with nursery'; 'Brownies' camps'; 'Terrible at clarinet, Grade 8'; 'Told at school to mime').

- Go on mapping your recollections and chart the complete journey of your musical life (or your development as a teacher) by recalling, listing and labelling each critical incident on each bend.

- Reflect on the whole picture and see what patterns start to emerge. Note where and when the watersheds, sudden swerves, turning points, currents, memorable moments or marker events occur in your development. This now becomes a navigable river representing a narrative of personal (and professional) significance that can, but does not necessarily have to, be sorted into a chronological sequence or an autobiographical timeline. The purpose is not necessarily to rearrange the pieces but rather to visualize and draw your own musical journey as a mighty winding river and to reflect upon what discoveries have marked your particular path (either as a musical learner or teacher). The technique of discovering emerging patterns of personal meaning within oneself and seeking and creating connections allows us to reflect upon the meanings of experiences in our past lives and potentially to set out on a new voyage.

We envisage Musical Pathways as an ongoing project, and to this end we are opening up a webpage on the NAME website where we will be posting, among other things, further musical pathways as an extension to this book. If you would like to contribute your own pathway, either as a written account or a 'river', please visit www.name.org.uk/publications.